RED SKY

A Dreamscape Press Anthology

Edited by
David Nell

DREAMSCAPE
PRESS

All Rights Reserved

This edition published in 2014 by
Dreamscape Press - United States of America

Without limiting the rights under copyright reserved above, no part of this publication may be reproduced, stored in or introduced into a retrieval system, or transmitted, in any form, or by any means (electronic, mechanical, photocopying, recording, or otherwise), without the prior written permission of both the copyright owner and the above publisher of this book.

If you purchased this book without a cover you should be aware that this book is stolen property. It was reported as "unsold and destroyed" to the publisher and neither the author nor the publisher has received any payment for this "stripped book."

Publisher's Note
These are works of fiction. Names, characters, places, and incidents either are the product of imagination or are used fictitiously, and any resemblance to actual persons, living or dead, business establishments, events, or locales is entirely coincidental.

First Printed 2014

ISBN: 1502939924

Copyrights: Assigned to Individual Authors

Website: dreamscapepress.wordpress.com
Twitter: twitter.com/dreamscapepress

Contents

Willy In The Nano Lab by Geoffrey A. Landis - Page 6

Cybernetic Sestina by E.S. Wynn - Page 7

Fatigue Of The Marionettes by Karen Neuberg - Page 9

The Fate Of Worlds by William Cullen, Jr. - Page 11

The Star-Treader by Clark Ashton Smith - Page 12

On This Outlying Planet by J.J. Steinfeld - Page 17

Close Encounters Of The Unique Kind by Adina Newman - Page 19

Redder Soil, Greener Grass by Sara Bickley - Page 21

Jabberwocky by Lewis Carroll - Page 22

Lost And Found by Fanni Sütő - Page 24

To No End Death by Seth Frederiksen - Page 25

Shine Down On Me by David Revilla - Page 28

Rain Check: version 36 by Chris Fradkin - Page 31

Songs From An Evil Wood by Edward Plunkett - Page 34

Aerial Corps Enlistment by David S. Pointer - Page 37

What The Robots Know by Alyssa Black - Page 38

The Raven by Edgar Allan Poe - Page 39

Flowing by Adrian George Nicolae - Page 44

You by Nora May French - Page 45

Pigeon Boy by Kyle Hemmings - Page 46

Repairman by John Grey - Page 47

Anastacia, Girl No. S10230 File: Insurgent by Carmen Tudor - Page 49

Rise Of The Machines by Stephanie Rose - Page 50

Goblin Market by Christina Rossetti - Page 52

Fungi From Yuggoth by H.P. Lovecraft - Page 70

The Landing by Matthew Wilson - Page 89

The Green Hills Of Earth by Robert A. Heinlein - Page 90

The Visitors by Ed Higgins - Page 92

Locksley Hall by Alfred Lord Tennyson - Page 94

The Stars Are Calling by Mathias Jansson - Page 99

Discombobulation by Rami Sebai - Page 101

Shadow Of Dreams by Robert E. Howard - Page 102

Armageddon by M.A. Crawford - Page 104

The Hosting Of The Sidhe by William Butler Yeats - Page 105

The Centaurs by Rudyard Kipling - Page 106

Lamia by John Keats - Page 108

Queen Mab by Percy Bysshe Shelley - Page 129

The Hunting Of The Dragon by G.K. Chesterton - Page 200

WILLY IN THE NANO LAB
Geoffrey A. Landis

Willy made a nano-critter,
set it on his little sister.
It dissolved her into goo,
reassembled her as a kangaroo.

Little Willy, oh so clever
put more nano-machines together.
Willy wasn't quite so smart:
they took Willy right apart.

It wasn't quite the thing to do;
dissolved his play-room into goo.
Now California's just goo that's gray
we didn't need it anyway.

Bio: Geoffrey A. Landis is a scientist, a science fiction writer, and a poet. As a scientist, he works at the NASA John Glenn Research Center on projects such as the Mars Exploration Rovers and developing new technologies for future space missions. As a science fiction writer, he has won the Hugo and Nebula awards, and is the author of one novel, Mars Crossing. As a poet, he has published poetry in numerous magazines and anthologies, and has twice won the Rhysling award for best science fiction poem, given out by the Science Fiction Poetry Association. More information can be found on his website, http://www.geoffreylandis.com.

CYBERNETIC SESTINA
E.S. Wynn

Racing lines of code awaken in my brain
Stir sleepy synapses interwoven with silicon
Trigger that first flutter of eyelids
That first deep breath
Before I armor myself with apps
Before I dive into the global network

I'm most at home in the digital infrastructure of the network
Where currents of data roar steadily through my brain
Sorted and categorized, scanned and shuffled by apps
Shunted along paths of mind-meat and silicon
Analyzed and absorbed by the dozens with each breath
Flying silently against the insides of my eyelids.

Ones, zeroes track in quick movements under eyelids.
When I am amidst the code, I am one with the network
I take in data, hold it, let it go with every breath
Change it with software and hardware at the edge of my brain
Send it back into the ocean of code and silicon
And scrape new data from the digital waves with my apps.

And I can catch some valuable code with my apps
Juicy leads, trends, tidbits and rumors fly under my eyelids
Carve hot paths through neuron and silicon
Crumbs of money, of prestige lost in the network
Picked up and shuffled, connected at the digital edges of my brain
Returned, offered, traded and sold with every breath.

All the while, I know my body is breathing, but I never feel my breath–

The breath of the waking world, I only feel the apps
As they take in new data, bring new code into my brain
Flicker it like a slide show under my eyelids
Here, in the digital world, I breathe only the code, the stuff of the network
And each inhale, each exhale is a sweet exchange between meat and silicon

There is freedom in the cold openness of the silicon.
I can feel it in every sensation, every touch, every breath
There is nothing in life like the network
No limbs or senses as quick or agile as my apps
No data as interesting as what moves under my eyelids
No light which burns as bright as the digital fire at the edges of my brain.

Oh, if only my mind were all silicon, my body all apps,
If only I could abandon the slow breath, the darkness of my eyelids
And live entirely in the light of the network, forever abandon the sluggish meat of my brain.

Bio: E.S. Wynn is the author of over 50 books in print and the chief editor of Thunderune Publishing.

FATIGUE OF THE MARIONETTES
Karen Neuberg

We reached up
fully expecting strings –
after all, we had been fooled before –
but this time we were really free,
as if the strings had turned into green snakes
who in old age devoured themselves.

Unspoken ideas,
which we had been dreaming of like promised toys,
filled our mouths –

filled them faster
than storm-driven sea
fingers its way inland.

And finally, we began to speak
and heard one another utter
ideas we'd never imagined
in throaty timbres that parsed thoughts like a curtain of forest
with intonations damp as a grove of mushrooms.

Until we held our ears against the din.

We tried to recall
what we once believed, recall the dream:

Even the most simple, self-ordained expression

would be a prayer.

We had been so sure it was the parables we played that held us bound.

Now that we speak and move
on our own, something has been forgotten;
and in our Great Council we debate
what it might be. We speak and speak
until our breath is wilted with heat.
We greet the turning of leaves and their return,
but are still no closer. On corners, some of us
simply hold out our hands;
but rain is the only miracle that touches.
Others make the pilgrimage
to cities where the strings are believed buried
in pits as large as Olympian pools.
They say they search for souvenirs,
that they will be sure to recognize what held us
straight and weightless
against this incessant pull,

this gravity.

*Fatigue of the Marionettes: Title of a watercolor by Man Ray, 1919

Bio: Karen Neuberg's poems have appeared in numerous online and print journals including Abstract Quill, Barrow Street, DIAGRAM, Forge, and Pirene's Fountain. Her chapbook, Detailed Still, was published by Poets Wear Prada and her chapbook, Myself Taking Stage, is forthcoming from Finishing Line Press. She's a five-time Pushcart and a Best of the Net nominee, holds an MFA from the New School, and is associate editor of First Literary Review-East. She lives in Brooklyn, NY.

THE FATE OF WORLDS
William Cullen, Jr.

A bat's swoop
blinks out some stars
ever so briefly
like an oracle revealing
where black holes will be.

Bio: William Cullen, Jr., is a veteran and works at a non-profit in Brooklyn, NY. His poetry has appeared in Asimov's Science Fiction Magazine, The Christian Science Monitor, Star*Line and other journals.

THE STAR-TREADER
Clark Ashton Smith

I.

A voice cried to me in a dawn of dreams,
Saying, "Make haste: the webs of death and birth
Are brushed away, and all the threads of earth
Wear to the breaking; spaceward gleams
Thine ancient pathway of the suns,
Whose flame is part of thee;
And deeps outreach immutably
Whose largeness runs
Through all thy spirit's mystery.
Go forth, and tread unharmed the blaze
Of stars where through thou camest in old days;
Pierce without fear each vast
Whose hugeness crushed thee not within the past.
A hand strikes off the chains of Time,
A hand swings back the door of years;
Now fall earth's bonds of gladness and of tears,
And opens the strait dream to space sublime."

II.

Who rides a dream, what hand shall stay!
What eye shall note or measure mete
His passage on a purpose fleet,
The thread and weaving of his way!
It caught me from the clasping world,
And swept beyond the brink of Sense,
My soul was flung, and poised, and whirled,

Like to a planet chained and hurled
With solar lightning strong and tense.
Swift as communicated rays
That leap from severed suns a gloom
Within whose waste no suns illume,
The wingèd dream fulfilled its ways.
Through years reversed and lit again
I followed that unending chain
Wherein the suns are links of light;
Retraced through lineal, ordered spheres
The twisting of the threads of years
In weavings wrought of noon and night;
Through stars and deeps I watched the dream unroll,
Those folds that form the raiment of the soul.

III.

Enkindling dawns of memory,
Each sun had radiance to relume
A sealed, disused, and darkened room
Within the soul's immensity.
Their alien ciphers shown and lit,
I understood what each had writ
Upon my spirit's scroll;
Again I wore mine ancient lives,
And knew the freedom and the gyves
That formed and marked my soul.

IV.

I delved in each forgotten mind,
The units that had builded me,
Whose deepnesses before were blind
And formless as infinity—
Knowing again each former world—
From planet unto planet whirled

Through gulfs that mightily divide
Like to an intervital sleep.
One world I found, where souls abide
Like winds that rest upon a rose;
Thereto they creep
To loose all burden of old woes.
And one I knew, where warp of pain
Is woven in the soul's attire;
And one, where with new loveliness
Is strengthened Beauty's olden chain—
Soft as a sound, and keen as fire—
In light no darkness may depress.

V.

Where no terrestrial dreams had trod
My vision entered undismayed,
And Life her hidden realms displayed
To me as to a curious god.
Where colored suns of systems triplicate
Bestow on planets weird, ineffable,
Green light that orbs them like an outer sea,
And large auroral noons that alternate
With skies like sunset held without abate,
Life's touch renewed incomprehensibly
The strains of mirth and grief's harmonious spell.
Dead passions like to stars relit
Shone in the gloom of ways forgot;
Where crownless gods in darkness sit
The day was full on altars hot.
I heard—once more a part of it—
The central music of the Pleiades,
And to Alcyone my soul
Swayed with the stars that own her song's control.
Unchallenged, glad I trod, a revenant
In worlds Edenic longly lost;

Or walked in spheres that sing to these,
O'er space no light has crossed,
Diverse as Hell's mad antiphone uptossed
To Heaven's angelic chant.

VI.

What vasts the dream went out to find!
I seemed beyond the world's recall
In gulfs where darkness is a wall
To render strong Antares blind!
In unimagined spheres I found
The sequence of my being's round—
Some life where firstling meed of Song,
The strange imperishable leaf,
Was placed on brows that starry Grief
Had crowned, and Pain anointed long;
Some avatar where Love
Sang like the last great star at morn
Ere Death filled all its sky;
Some life in fresher years unworn
Upon a world whereof
Peace was a robe like to the calms that lie
On pools aglow with latter spring:
There Life's pellucid surface took
Clear image of all things, nor shook
Till touch of Death's obscuring wing;
Some earlier awakening
In pristine years, when giant strife
Of forces darkly whirled
First forged the thing called Life—
Hot from the furnace of the suns—
Upon the anvil of a world.

VII.

Thus knew I those anterior ones
Whose lives in mine were blent;
Till, lo! my dream, that held a night
Where Rigel sends no word of might,
Was emptied of the trodden stars,
And dwindled to the sun's extent—
The brain's familiar prison-bars,
And raiment of the sorrow and the mirth
Wrought by the shuttles intricate of earth.

Bio: Clark Ashton Smith was a poet, sculptor, painter and author of fantasy, horror and science fiction short stories. Smith spent most of his life in the small town of Auburn, California, living in a small cabin with his parents, Fanny and Timeus Smith. His formal education was limited: he attended only eight years of grammar school and never went to high school. However, he continued to teach himself after he left school, learning French and Spanish, and his near-photographic memory allowed him to retain prodigious amounts from his very wide reading, including several entire dictionaries and encyclopedias.

ON THIS OUTLYING PLANET
J. J. Steinfeld

Here I am on this outlying planet
no name yet
but nameless things
especially planets
always irritate
and naming must be done
like breathing or complaining
about eternal things.

The trip wasn't so bad
not like in sci-fi films.
Should I remove my spacesuit
breathe the air of this outlying planet?
It could be purer or worse
than my previous planet
but why take a chance
my spacesuit is state of the art
and I have a lifetime supply
of the best manufactured air
money can buy.

Maybe I won't leave my spacecraft
maybe I will sit here
with my protective spacesuit
and look through the portal
at this outlying planet
no longer outlying
because I am finally here.

Maybe I will name it *Earth*
or *Imagination*
or leave it nameless
I am not sure yet
being new to space travel
and landing on outlying planets.

Bio: J. J. Steinfeld is a Canadian fiction writer, poet, and playwright who lives on Prince Edward Island, where he is patiently waiting for the arrival of a spacecraft from a distant planet. While waiting, he has published fourteen books, including Anton Chekhov Was Never in Charlottetown *(Stories, Gaspereau Press),* Would You Hide Me? *(Stories, Gaspereau Press),* An Affection for Precipices *(Poetry, Serengeti Press),* Misshapenness *(Poetry, Ekstasis Editions), and* A Glass Shard and Memory *(Stories, Recliner Books). His short stories and poems have appeared in numerous anthologies and periodicals internationally, and over forty of his one-act plays and a handful of full-length plays have been performed in Canada and the United States, but none yet on any other planet.*

CLOSE ENCOUNTERS OF THE UNIQUE KIND
Adina Newman

I stand in the shadows
of an out of body experience.

My disguise fits firmly
too perfectly
a little snug
blending me in
keeping me invisible
masking the alien that lies beneath

I feel I might crash land.

I could look to the stars
make a wish
wait for a mothership
to beam me up
abduct me
whisk me away to planets unknown

But I won't.

Instead,
I choose to remain
on Earth
a whole world to invade

objects unidentified
a planet upon which to take flight
and leave my legacy.

Bio: Adina Newman's poems have appeared in Enchanted Conversation, The Camel Saloon, Yes, Poetry, Eunoia Review, Poetica Magazine, and other print and electronic publications. She lives in the Washington, D.C. area with her husband and pet snake.

REDDER SOIL, GREENER GRASS
Sara Bickley

My father used to take me out
on shirtsleeve summer nights
to point out the arrangement of the stars.
He showed me planets, red and white;
the red one was my favorite sight.
I longed to go to Mars.

I take my daughter out sometimes
on greatcoat Martian nights
to point the silent stars out as they gleam.
Of all the planets, blue and white,
the bluest is her best delight
and Earth-life is her dream.

Bio: Sara Bickley's poetry has recently appeared or is forthcoming in *Punchnel's*, *Paper Crow*, and *Trinacria*, among other publications. She is a student at the University of Montana.

JABBERWOCKY
Lewis Carroll

'Twas brillig, and the slithy toves
Did gyre and gimble in the wabe;
All mimsy were the borogoves,
And the mome raths outgrabe.

"Beware the Jabberwock, my son
The jaws that bite, the claws that catch!
Beware the Jubjub bird, and shun
The frumious Bandersnatch!"

He took his vorpal sword in hand;
Long time the manxome foe he sought—
So rested he by the Tumtum tree,
And stood awhile in thought.

And, as in uffish thought he stood,
The Jabberwock, with eyes of flame,
Came whiffling through the tulgey wood,
And burbled as it came!

One, two! One, two! And through and through
The vorpal blade went snicker-snack!
He left it dead, and with its head
He went galumphing back.

"And hast thou slain the Jabberwock?
Come to my arms, my beamish boy!
O frabjous day! Callooh! Callay!"
He chortled in his joy.

'Twas brillig, and the slithy toves
Did gyre and gimble in the wabe;
All mimsy were the borogoves,
And the mome raths outgrabe.

Bio: Lewis Carroll was the pen name of Charles L. Dodgson, author of the children's classics "Alice's Adventures in Wonderland" and "Through the Looking-Glass."

LOST AND FOUND
Fanni Sütő

My love was lost in a swirl of time
When we travelled through the past

My love was lost in a twirl of space
When we journeyed past the stars

My love was found in a pile of books
When I dove into the pages

My love was found in a broken dream
When I finally woke up.

Bio: Fanni Sütő is a 23-year old writer of everything she can lay a hand on; be it poems, flash fiction, novels or anything you can imagine. She has been writing in her mother tongue (Hungarian) for a good ten years and started to come up with stories in English since the beginning of 2013. Her favorite genres are urban fantasy, fairy tale reworks and magical realism. She has been published in various online magazines and e-journals magazines such as Tincture Journal, Enchanted Conversations or The Casket of Fictional Delights and in the Haiku of the Dead collection of Dreamscape Press.

TO NO END DEATH
Seth Frederiksen

Thunder of the ion cannons,
Roar in the distance.
The true music of the battlefield.
The boom of the guns,
The crack shock of the impact.
It is surpassed only in the morbid glory,
By the screams of the dead and the dying.
They are spared from the horrors
That are to come tonight.
Each strike, every explosion
That is sounded alerts us all,
How the hour soon draws near.
When man and steel and death become one.
Upon the lunar-death ground of a distant world,
Once fertile and promising with hope and life.
We, man, have made it a hell, forever.
Officers cry out to men of the watch,
"Shoot the cowards! All to the front!"
They should know us now.
We will not run.
We will not hide.
We will die as men must all die.
The lines of the laureate run through my mind.
A ghost of a past long gone,
Whispering in my ear,
"Theirs was not to make reply,
Theirs was not to reason why,
Theirs was but to do and die."
Die, die, die we will.

With rifle in hand,
Sword unsheathed,
And argon-bayonet pointing,
Steadfast and true, to the front.
We will charge,
We will be butchered,
We will be slaughtered.
For the eternal glory of God,
For the honor of king and country,
For the purity of family and paramours,
For the virtue of teachers and friends.
Though they will never know,
suffering they are spared.
How can they know, how can they ever know?
The living nightmares we face for them.
Few will ever know our fate.
None will come to see our graves.
Only those who fall beside us,
They will be our company.
We finally hear the call made at last.
Trumpets and drums pollute the air.
Over the top, we climb up.
Barrage of the energy guns
And shellfire rake our lines.
But onward we march.
Barbed wire tear our flesh.
Gas floods our lungs.
Forward we charge.
Calvary train their lances.
Infantry hone their guns.
The enemy meet us now,
Upon this field of death.
Fusion fighters swirl around another,
Endlessly in the heavens.
Bombs, blasters, missiles;
All lighting up the night sky.

None dare to give the field,
None but the dead.
None never seek to yield,
None but the dead.
All fight with all their might,
All fight for reasons to survive.
In the end, both sides return,
To their old trench lines.
And the rains soon fall from cloudless skies,
Lightly cleaning the dead.
The lights dwindle from the fighter jets,
Replaced by god's light above.
No victor is claimed but death itself,
Its harvest come to fruition.
The war goes ever on and on,
Only the dead seeing its end.

Bio: Seth Frederiksen is currently living in North Carolina, but is originally from Southern California. He earned his bachelor's with honors in history at North Carolina State University last year and is currently working on his master's through the University of Nebraska at Kearney. He has been published in Red E-zine and Haiku of the Dead.

SHINE DOWN ON ME
David Revilla

On a world choked by fire,
the final odyssey of man is about to begin.
The clouds an angry orange as ships take to the sky,
their engines overshadowed by the sound of the approaching storm.

The last storm.

I wait here,
the last man on a doomed planet,
waiting for the inevitable end to come.
For it is not just my end,
but the end of ten-thousand years of history.

The world of my ancestors trembles beneath me,
cowering in the face of the doomed star.
Once our protector,
it has turned on us like a feral dog,
once loyal and now snapping at the one thing it used to protect.

The ships are all gone now.
Everyone is gone.
I am all that's left of a once-thriving civilization.

I stand on that last hill,
my skin aflame with a kiss of fire,
my eyes darkened by perpetual light,
knowing this is the end.

A relic is what I am.

This planet and everything on it,
myself included,
are of a lost age.
A forgotten age.

Now it is time for all of us to die.

I embrace this fate,
the way a mother spider would her last moments,
as her children devoured her,
knowing her death would mean that they continued living.
With me die all my prejudices,
my ignorance,
my hatred,
my fears.

With those ships go the best of humanity,
the best of me.
I embrace the fire,
and so too does the earth.

It is shining now.
The light at the end of my tunnel.
May it consume me entirely,
for my spirit burns brighter still on this,
the last hill on earth.

So warm.

Who knew the end would be so warm?

Bio: David Revilla is a freelance writer with degrees in both English and Publishing. In addition to having short stories published in Siren's Call Magazine

and Dreamscape Press, he has completed his first novel, "The River Styx', which can be found on his website, darev.weebly.com.

RAIN CHECK: version 36
Chris Fradkin

Aldous looked outside the window.
It was black.
The sky up on the wall said 7:30.
AM, PM?
He didn't really know.

Aldous looked outside the window. Later.
Everything was broken.
Twisted inside-out. Reflections of reflections on the wall.
He shrugged.
He looked inside his keep box.
A spool of yarn. A nickel. A pendant from his dad.
He pushed the box back underneath his bed.

Aldous looked outside— Was it the next day or the next?
He really didn't care or think about it.
A centipede was crawling on the awning.
Aldous counted all the footsteps that it made.
Nine-hundred ninety-nine and seven thousand.
Hmm, he thought. He counted them once more and then again.

Aldous looked outside the window.
It was daylight.
He blinked.
The program indicator turned to night.
Aldous blinked again.
The program turned to daylight.
Aldous blinked once more.
The lights outside went out.

Dark— The world outside and in.
Evelyn left cookies on the sideboard.
Darren left his wallet on the— Where'd he leave his wallet?
Wellwish sang, he said. His nails were growing longer.

Aldous looked outside the window.
It was winter-time and blue.
It was time, he thought.
The footsteps drawing closer.
Three knocks upon the door.
No 'who is it?' from his end.
His lungs gave out in rueful admonition.

A woman's voice rang silently.
All colors pooled to red.
Was it winter? Was it spring for wayward chickens?
He pondered till the evening. He made peace.
He pulled the curtain.
That looks right, he said.

Aldous looked outside the window.
Waves of traffic sang below.
His father gave a speech on restitution.
Here, here, Adelphin offered.
Here's his hand. He said he's sorry.
Aldous tumbled through the cellophane disposal.

While the traffic kept on churning.
While Ezalandro played his part.
While Alessandra's puppy bit the postman.
Aldous reached inside his keep box.
He tendered a balloon.
He held it to his mouth. He blew.

Bio: Chris Fradkin is a beet farmer who is tending crops in Central California. His prose and poetry have appeared in Thrice Fiction, Monkeybicycle, and Thrush Poetry Journal. His songs have been performed by Fergie, The Plimsouls, and The Flamin' Groovies. His photography has appeared in Bartleby Snopes, and his Emmy-award-winning sound editorial has graced The X-Files.

SONGS FROM AN EVIL WOOD
Edward Plunkett

I.

There is no wrath in the stars,
They do not rage in the sky;
I look from the evil wood
And find myself wondering why.

Why do they not scream out
And grapple star against star,
Seeking for blood in the wood,
As all things round me are?

They do not glare like the sky
Or flash like the deeps of the wood;
But they shine softly on
In their sacred solitude.

To their happy haunts
Silence from us has flown,
She whom we loved of old
And know it now she is gone.

When will she come again
Though for one second only?
She whom we loved is gone
And the whole world is lonely.

And the elder giants come
Sometimes, tramping from far,

Through the weird and flickering light
Made by an earthly star.

And the giant with his club,
And the dwarf with rage in his breath,
And the elder giants from far,
They are the children of Death.

They are all abroad to-night
And are breaking the hills with their brood,
And the birds are all asleep,
Even in Plugstreet Wood.

II.

Somewhere lost in the haze
The sun goes down in the cold,
And birds in this evil wood
Chirrup home as of old;

Chirrup, stir and are still,
On the high twigs frozen and thin.
There is no more noise of them now,
And the long night sets in.

Of all the wonderful things
That I have seen in the wood,
I marvel most at the birds,
At their chirp and their quietude.

For a giant smites with his club
All day the tops of the hill,
Sometimes he rests at night,
Oftener he beats them still.

And a dwarf with a grim black mane

Raps with repeated rage
All night in the valley below
On the wooden walls of his cage.

III.

I met with Death in his country,
With his scythe and his hollow eye
Walking the roads of Belgium.
I looked and he passed me by.

Since he passed me by in Plug Street,
In the wood of the evil name,
I shall not now lie with the heroes,
I shall not share their fame;

I shall never be as they are,
A name in the land of the Free,
Since I looked on Death in Flanders
And he did not look at me.

Bio: Edward John Moreton Drax Plunkett, 18th Baron of Dunsany was an Irish writer and dramatist, notable for his work, mostly in fantasy, published under the name Lord Dunsany.

AERIAL CORPS ENLISTMENT
David S. Pointer

The space recruiters
arrived at the playgrounds
wearing airship captain
aftershave scanning kids'
brain microchips to replace
the old aptitude tests showing
which applicants could excel
in underworld galaxies above
us who could navigate primal
eternity inside burning worm-
holes wearing tan snakeskin
shenanigans and bigger smiles
grateful for the opportunity
to never jet beam on back.

Bio: David S. Pointer has recent poems in "Indiana Horror" 2013 anthology. His most recent poetry book is entitled "Oncoming Crime Facts" sold through www.lulu.com. David also has recent horror poetry for youth included in "Bleed" anthology. "Bleed" is a charity anthology to raise money for young cancer patients.

WHAT THE ROBOTS KNOW
Alyssa Black

In my mind, I've always pictured Mark Mothersbaugh to secretly be a robot from outer space. He travelled to earth in the 1970's to warn us about our actions. *"We are all De-evolution"*, he warned. Some of us listened, a lot didn't. In 2010, DEVO returned with a new message about nature and the human responsibility to take care of earth. Hopefully, humans will heed this warning. If we do not, we have no one to blame but ourselves.

Bio: Alyssa Black is a comic book enthusiast who drives a bright green car. She attends school at IU Northwest.

THE RAVEN
Edgar Allan Poe

Once upon a midnight dreary, while I pondered, weak and weary,
Over many a quaint and curious volume of forgotten lore,
While I nodded, nearly napping, suddenly there came a tapping,
As of some one gently rapping, rapping at my chamber door.
"Tis some visitor,' I muttered, 'tapping at my chamber door-
Only this, and nothing more.'

Ah, distinctly I remember it was in the bleak December,
And each separate dying ember wrought its ghost upon the floor.
Eagerly I wished the morrow;- vainly I had sought to borrow
From my books surcease of sorrow- sorrow for the lost Lenore-
For the rare and radiant maiden whom the angels name Lenore-
Nameless here for evermore.

And the silken sad uncertain rustling of each purple curtain
Thrilled me- filled me with fantastic terrors never felt before;
So that now, to still the beating of my heart, I stood repeating,
"Tis some visitor entreating entrance at my chamber door-
Some late visitor entreating entrance at my chamber door;-
This it is, and nothing more.'

Presently my soul grew stronger; hesitating then no longer,
'Sir,' said I, 'or Madam, truly your forgiveness I implore;
But the fact is I was napping, and so gently you came rapping,
And so faintly you came tapping, tapping at my chamber door,
That I scarce was sure I heard you'- here I opened wide the door;-
Darkness there, and nothing more.

Deep into that darkness peering, long I stood there wondering,

fearing,
Doubting, dreaming dreams no mortals ever dared to dream before;
But the silence was unbroken, and the stillness gave no token,
And the only word there spoken was the whispered word, 'Lenore!'
This I whispered, and an echo murmured back the word, 'Lenore!'-
Merely this, and nothing more.

Back into the chamber turning, all my soul within me burning,
Soon again I heard a tapping somewhat louder than before.
'Surely,' said I, 'surely that is something at my window lattice:
Let me see, then, what thereat is, and this mystery explore-
Let my heart be still a moment and this mystery explore;-
'Tis the wind and nothing more.'

Open here I flung the shutter, when, with many a flirt and flutter,
In there stepped a stately raven of the saintly days of yore;
Not the least obeisance made he; not a minute stopped or stayed he;
But, with mien of lord or lady, perched above my chamber door-
Perched upon a bust of Pallas just above my chamber door-
Perched, and sat, and nothing more.

Then this ebony bird beguiling my sad fancy into smiling,
By the grave and stern decorum of the countenance it wore.
'Though thy crest be shorn and shaven, thou,' I said, 'art sure no craven,
Ghastly grim and ancient raven wandering from the Nightly shore-
Tell me what thy lordly name is on the Night's Plutonian shore!'
Quoth the Raven, 'Nevermore.'

Much I marvelled this ungainly fowl to hear discourse so plainly,
Though its answer little meaning- little relevancy bore;
For we cannot help agreeing that no living human being
Ever yet was blest with seeing bird above his chamber door-
Bird or beast upon the sculptured bust above his chamber door,

With such name as 'Nevermore.'

But the raven, sitting lonely on the placid bust, spoke only
That one word, as if his soul in that one word he did outpour.
Nothing further then he uttered- not a feather then he fluttered-
Till I scarcely more than muttered, 'other friends have flown before-
On the morrow he will leave me, as my hopes have flown before.'
Then the bird said, 'Nevermore.'

Startled at the stillness broken by reply so aptly spoken,
'Doubtless,' said I, 'what it utters is its only stock and store,
Caught from some unhappy master whom unmerciful Disaster
Followed fast and followed faster till his songs one burden bore-
Till the dirges of his Hope that melancholy burden bore
Of 'Never- nevermore'.'

But the Raven still beguiling all my fancy into smiling,
Straight I wheeled a cushioned seat in front of bird, and bust and door;
Then upon the velvet sinking, I betook myself to linking
Fancy unto fancy, thinking what this ominous bird of yore-
What this grim, ungainly, ghastly, gaunt and ominous bird of yore
Meant in croaking 'Nevermore.'

This I sat engaged in guessing, but no syllable expressing
To the fowl whose fiery eyes now burned into my bosom's core;
This and more I sat divining, with my head at ease reclining
On the cushion's velvet lining that the lamplight gloated o'er,
But whose velvet violet lining with the lamplight gloating o'er,
She shall press, ah, nevermore!

Then methought the air grew denser, perfumed from an unseen censer
Swung by Seraphim whose footfalls tinkled on the tufted floor.
'Wretch,' I cried, 'thy God hath lent thee- by these angels he

hath sent thee
Respite- respite and nepenthe, from thy memories of Lenore!
Quaff, oh quaff this kind nepenthe and forget this lost Lenore!'
Quoth the Raven, 'Nevermore.'

'Prophet!' said I, 'thing of evil!- prophet still, if bird or devil!-
Whether Tempter sent, or whether tempest tossed thee here ashore,
Desolate yet all undaunted, on this desert land enchanted-
On this home by horror haunted- tell me truly, I implore-
Is there- is there balm in Gilead?- tell me- tell me, I implore!'
Quoth the Raven, 'Nevermore.'

'Prophet!' said I, 'thing of evil- prophet still, if bird or devil!
By that Heaven that bends above us- by that God we both adore-
Tell this soul with sorrow laden if, within the distant Aidenn,
It shall clasp a sainted maiden whom the angels name Lenore-
Clasp a rare and radiant maiden whom the angels name Lenore.'
Quoth the Raven, 'Nevermore.'

'Be that word our sign in parting, bird or fiend,' I shrieked, upstarting-
'Get thee back into the tempest and the Night's Plutonian shore!
Leave no black plume as a token of that lie thy soul hath spoken!
Leave my loneliness unbroken!- quit the bust above my door!
Take thy beak from out my heart, and take thy form from off my door!'
Quoth the Raven, 'Nevermore.'

And the Raven, never flitting, still is sitting, still is sitting
On the pallid bust of Pallas just above my chamber door;
And his eyes have all the seeming of a demon's that is dreaming,
And the lamplight o'er him streaming throws his shadow on the floor;
And my soul from out that shadow that lies floating on the floor

Shall be lifted- nevermore!

Bio: The name Poe brings to mind images of murderers and madmen, premature burials, and mysterious women who return from the dead. His works have been in print since 1827 and include such literary classics as "The Tell-Tale Heart," "The Raven," and "The Fall of the House of Usher." This versatile writer's oeuvre includes short stories, poetry, a novel, a textbook, a book of scientific theory, and hundreds of essays and book reviews. He is widely acknowledged as the inventor of the modern detective story and an innovator in the science fiction genre, but he made his living as America's first great literary critic and theoretician. Poe's reputation today rests primarily on his tales of terror as well as on his haunting lyric poetry. Just as the bizarre characters in Poe's stories have captured the public imagination so too has Poe himself. He is seen as a morbid, mysterious figure lurking in the shadows of moonlit cemeteries or crumbling castles. This is the Poe of legend. But much of what we know about Poe is wrong, the product of a biography written by one of his enemies in an attempt to defame the author's name. The real Poe was born to traveling actors in Boston on January 19, 1809. Edgar was the second of three children. His other brother William Henry Leonard Poe would also become a poet before his early death, and Poe's sister Rosalie Poe would grow up to teach penmanship at a Richmond girls' school. Within three years of Poe's birth both of his parents had died, and he was taken in by the wealthy tobacco merchant John Allan and his wife Frances Valentine Allan in Richmond, Virginia while Poe's siblings went to live with other families. Mr. Allan would rear Poe to be a businessman and a Virginia gentleman, but Poe had dreams of being a writer in emulation of his childhood hero the British poet Lord Byron. Early poetic verses found written in a young Poe's handwriting on the backs of Allan's ledger sheets reveal how little interest Poe had in the tobacco business.

FLOWING
Adrian George Nicolae

Mountain peaks turn into needless
Oceans and seas meld with the green.
I fly through marshmallowey clouds
On my way to the dark sky.

This sixteen-year old girl
soaring through, to space.
Youngest ever, so they say.
Smartest? Not by a long shot.

Ever since I was a child
I dreamed about the moon
Jumping on its soil, making
Sand castles held together with toothpicks.

A star is passing us by
Leaving its golden trail
Flowing behind, like ours is
Straying from Earth, for good.

Bio: Adrian George Nicolae hails from Bucharest, Romania. He writes dark, bizarre stories and poems with a touch of humor.

YOU
Nora May French

All elfish woodland things that Fancy broods–
The comrades of my solitary moods–
Would crouch when heavy footsteps passed them by,
And peer from shelter–freakish folk and shy.

At you they pricked their furry ears in doubt;
Then, "This one sees–he knows!" they cried.
"Come out!"
They thought to hush their piping till you passed.
"Come out!" they cried. "We dare be brave at last!"

So forth their gay procession sways and weaves;
And some are crowned with roses, some with leaves,
And all are mine, but some I never knew.
I could not wake them, but they come for you.

Bio: Nora May French was a California poet and member of the bohemian literary circles of the Carmel Arts and Crafts Club which flourished after the Great San Francisco Earthquake and Fire of 1906. Although many of her poems celebrate the serenity of coastal landscape, others are less sanguine: they offer glimpses into the mind of a young woman torn between pressure to submit to social roles and longing to live creatively. "All sensible people will ultimately be damned," she said, but lack of stability also plagued her.

PIGEON BOY
Kyle Hemmings

When he first learned he could fly, Pigeon-boy blushed
at the thought of hand-me-down wings. Yet, he learned
to dance on street corners, laugh mid-stream
at the thought of being lighter than an idea.
Then he was hired to carry messages between lovers.
The distances increased & Pigeon-boy grew breathless.
Sometimes, he delivered messages to the wrong lovers.
The notes read *I love you, still*, or *walking on air*.
Some receivers at the wrong destinations died
in air-tight bliss. When this happened,
the world grew smaller. One day, a morning
where everyone carried some form of artificial sunshine
in their pockets, of paper planes released from the sweaty palms
of air controllers, Pigeon-boy delivered a note that read:
I don't love you anymore. He fell from the sky.
A girl named Yugi took him home, brought him back to life
with her songs of flight. From then on, Pigeon-boy was wiser
with air-time, more cautious about his fly-ways. He circled
& landed only within her. In total, they never touched ground.
Whenever she breaks open a Chinese cookie,
the message is always the same – *When the world is cold, stay indoors.*

Bio: *Kyle Hemmings lives and works in New Jersey. He has been published in Elimae, Smokelong Quarterly, This Zine Will Change Your Life, Blaze Vox, Matchbook, and elsewhere. He loves 50s Sci-Fi movies, manga comics, and pre-punk garage bands of the 60s.*

REPAIRMAN
John Grey

It's the world's first
billion dollar service call

out of deep sleep,
in a metal womb,
seven feet long, four feet high,
computer screen dropping Earth
like a blue lead weight,
hovering amid plastic pouches
fall of familiar books,
a diary, personal belongings,
scientific equipment,
all geared to reel that planet back in
on memory's ropes and chains

six months of this,
occasional calls home,
daily face to face
with photographs,
mein host of dead satellites
needing resuscitation,
telescopes requiring tweaking…
his space age train set,
days, nights,
all scientific handiwork,
in a vast universe
as confining as pneumatic walls

no gravity,

just floating,
but isolation, loneliness,
gravity as he knows it

Bio: John Grey is an Australian born poet. Recently published in International Poetry Review, Vallum and the science fiction anthology, "The Kennedy Curse" with work upcoming in Bryant Literary Magazine, Natural Bridge and the Pedestal.

ANASTACIA, GIRL No. S10230
File: INSURGENT

Carmen Tudor

This is the last night she'll ever know Earth
They're deleting her file. They're shutting her down
But she's brave, not like me. She's not scared of death.
This is the last night she'll ever know Earth.
They laugh as they work and rupture her last circuit
She's quieter now – her memories have gone.
This is the last night she'll ever know Earth
They're deleting her file. They're shutting her down

Bio: Carmen Tudor's young adult fiction appears in various international anthologies and journals including Real Girls Don't Rust, Spotlight, and Spirited: 13 Haunting Tales. Find her online at carmentudor.net and @carmen_tudor. She lives in Melbourne, Australia.

RISE OF THE MACHINES
Stephanie Rose

The city is deserted
Silent
Desolate
Nothing but the occasional clank
Metallic
Or the hissing whoosh of steam.
The city is in ruins
Ravaged
Neglected
No more need to maintain homes
Abandoned
Left to their slow destruction.
The city is in darkness
Chilling
Isolated
The new residents need no light
Unseeing
Yet omnipresent in the shadows.
The machines rose swiftly
Sudden
Unexpected
Humanity stood no chance
Vulnerable
Brought down by their own creation.

Bio: Stephanie Rose is a marine biologist and is currently studying aquatic

pathobiology in Scotland. She is, however, very passionate about writing and loves to write both fiction and poetry.

GOBLIN MARKET
Christina Rossetti

Morning and evening
Maids heard the goblins cry:
"Come buy our orchard fruits,
Come buy, come buy:
Apples and quinces,
Lemons and oranges,
Plump unpeck'd cherries,
Melons and raspberries,
Bloom-down-cheek'd peaches,
Swart-headed mulberries,
Wild free-born cranberries,
Crab-apples, dewberries,
Pine-apples, blackberries,
Apricots, strawberries;—
All ripe together
In summer weather,—
Morns that pass by,
Fair eves that fly;
Come buy, come buy:
Our grapes fresh from the vine,
Pomegranates full and fine,
Dates and sharp bullaces,
Rare pears and greengages,
Damsons and bilberries,
Taste them and try:
Currants and gooseberries,
Bright-fire-like barberries,
Figs to fill your mouth,
Citrons from the South,

Sweet to tongue and sound to eye;
Come buy, come buy."

Evening by evening
Among the brookside rushes,
Laura bow'd her head to hear,
Lizzie veil'd her blushes:
Crouching close together
In the cooling weather,
With clasping arms and cautioning lips,
With tingling cheeks and finger tips.
"Lie close," Laura said,
Pricking up her golden head:
"We must not look at goblin men,
We must not buy their fruits:
Who knows upon what soil they fed
Their hungry thirsty roots?"
"Come buy," call the goblins
Hobbling down the glen.

"Oh," cried Lizzie, "Laura, Laura,
You should not peep at goblin men."
Lizzie cover'd up her eyes,
Cover'd close lest they should look;
Laura rear'd her glossy head,
And whisper'd like the restless brook:
"Look, Lizzie, look, Lizzie,
Down the glen tramp little men.
One hauls a basket,
One bears a plate,
One lugs a golden dish
Of many pounds weight.
How fair the vine must grow
Whose grapes are so luscious;
How warm the wind must blow
Through those fruit bushes."

"No," said Lizzie, "No, no, no;
Their offers should not charm us,
Their evil gifts would harm us."
She thrust a dimpled finger
In each ear, shut eyes and ran:
Curious Laura chose to linger
Wondering at each merchant man.
One had a cat's face,
One whisk'd a tail,
One tramp'd at a rat's pace,
One crawl'd like a snail,
One like a wombat prowl'd obtuse and furry,
One like a ratel tumbled hurry skurry.
She heard a voice like voice of doves
Cooing all together:
They sounded kind and full of loves
In the pleasant weather.

Laura stretch'd her gleaming neck
Like a rush-imbedded swan,
Like a lily from the beck,
Like a moonlit poplar branch,
Like a vessel at the launch
When its last restraint is gone.

Backwards up the mossy glen
Turn'd and troop'd the goblin men,
With their shrill repeated cry,
"Come buy, come buy."
When they reach'd where Laura was
They stood stock still upon the moss,
Leering at each other,
Brother with queer brother;
Signalling each other,
Brother with sly brother.
One set his basket down,

One rear'd his plate;
One began to weave a crown
Of tendrils, leaves, and rough nuts brown
(Men sell not such in any town);
One heav'd the golden weight
Of dish and fruit to offer her:
"Come buy, come buy," was still their cry.
Laura stared but did not stir,
Long'd but had no money:
The whisk-tail'd merchant bade her taste
In tones as smooth as honey,
The cat-faced purr'd,
The rat-faced spoke a word
Of welcome, and the snail-paced even was heard;
One parrot-voiced and jolly
Cried "Pretty Goblin" still for "Pretty Polly;"—
One whistled like a bird.

But sweet-tooth Laura spoke in haste:
"Good folk, I have no coin;
To take were to purloin:
I have no copper in my purse,
I have no silver either,
And all my gold is on the furze
That shakes in windy weather
Above the rusty heather."
"You have much gold upon your head,"
They answer'd all together:
"Buy from us with a golden curl."
She clipp'd a precious golden lock,
She dropp'd a tear more rare than pearl,
Then suck'd their fruit globes fair or red:
Sweeter than honey from the rock,
Stronger than man-rejoicing wine,
Clearer than water flow'd that juice;
She never tasted such before,

How should it cloy with length of use?
She suck'd and suck'd and suck'd the more
Fruits which that unknown orchard bore;
She suck'd until her lips were sore;
Then flung the emptied rinds away
But gather'd up one kernel stone,
And knew not was it night or day
As she turn'd home alone.

Lizzie met her at the gate
Full of wise upbraidings:
"Dear, you should not stay so late,
Twilight is not good for maidens;
Should not loiter in the glen
In the haunts of goblin men.
Do you not remember Jeanie,
How she met them in the moonlight,
Took their gifts both choice and many,
Ate their fruits and wore their flowers
Pluck'd from bowers
Where summer ripens at all hours?
But ever in the noonlight
She pined and pined away;
Sought them by night and day,
Found them no more, but dwindled and grew grey;
Then fell with the first snow,
While to this day no grass will grow
Where she lies low:
I planted daisies there a year ago
That never blow.
You should not loiter so."
"Nay, hush," said Laura:
"Nay, hush, my sister:
I ate and ate my fill,
Yet my mouth waters still;
To-morrow night I will

Buy more;" and kiss'd her:
"Have done with sorrow;
I'll bring you plums to-morrow
Fresh on their mother twigs,
Cherries worth getting;
You cannot think what figs
My teeth have met in,
What melons icy-cold
Piled on a dish of gold
Too huge for me to hold,
What peaches with a velvet nap,
Pellucid grapes without one seed:
Odorous indeed must be the mead
Whereon they grow, and pure the wave they drink
With lilies at the brink,
And sugar-sweet their sap."

Golden head by golden head,
Like two pigeons in one nest
Folded in each other's wings,
They lay down in their curtain'd bed:
Like two blossoms on one stem,
Like two flakes of new-fall'n snow,
Like two wands of ivory
Tipp'd with gold for awful kings.
Moon and stars gaz'd in at them,
Wind sang to them lullaby,
Lumbering owls forbore to fly,
Not a bat flapp'd to and fro
Round their rest:
Cheek to cheek and breast to breast
Lock'd together in one nest.

Early in the morning
When the first cock crow'd his warning,
Neat like bees, as sweet and busy,

Laura rose with Lizzie:
Fetch'd in honey, milk'd the cows,
Air'd and set to rights the house,
Kneaded cakes of whitest wheat,
Cakes for dainty mouths to eat,
Next churn'd butter, whipp'd up cream,
Fed their poultry, sat and sew'd;
Talk'd as modest maidens should:
Lizzie with an open heart,
Laura in an absent dream,
One content, one sick in part;
One warbling for the mere bright day's delight,
One longing for the night.

At length slow evening came:
They went with pitchers to the reedy brook;
Lizzie most placid in her look,
Laura most like a leaping flame.
They drew the gurgling water from its deep;
Lizzie pluck'd purple and rich golden flags,
Then turning homeward said: "The sunset flushes
Those furthest loftiest crags;
Come, Laura, not another maiden lags.
No wilful squirrel wags,
The beasts and birds are fast asleep."
But Laura loiter'd still among the rushes
And said the bank was steep.

And said the hour was early still
The dew not fall'n, the wind not chill;
Listening ever, but not catching
The customary cry,
"Come buy, come buy,"
With its iterated jingle
Of sugar-baited words:
Not for all her watching

Once discerning even one goblin
Racing, whisking, tumbling, hobbling;
Let alone the herds
That used to tramp along the glen,
In groups or single,
Of brisk fruit-merchant men.

Till Lizzie urged, "O Laura, come;
I hear the fruit-call but I dare not look:
You should not loiter longer at this brook:
Come with me home.
The stars rise, the moon bends her arc,
Each glowworm winks her spark,
Let us get home before the night grows dark:
For clouds may gather
Though this is summer weather,
Put out the lights and drench us through;
Then if we lost our way what should we do?"

Laura turn'd cold as stone
To find her sister heard that cry alone,
That goblin cry,
"Come buy our fruits, come buy."
Must she then buy no more such dainty fruit?
Must she no more such succous pasture find,
Gone deaf and blind?
Her tree of life droop'd from the root:
She said not one word in her heart's sore ache;
But peering thro' the dimness, nought discerning,
Trudg'd home, her pitcher dripping all the way;
So crept to bed, and lay
Silent till Lizzie slept;
Then sat up in a passionate yearning,
And gnash'd her teeth for baulk'd desire, and wept
As if her heart would break.

Day after day, night after night,
Laura kept watch in vain
In sullen silence of exceeding pain.
She never caught again the goblin cry:
"Come buy, come buy;"—
She never spied the goblin men
Hawking their fruits along the glen:
But when the noon wax'd bright
Her hair grew thin and grey;
She dwindled, as the fair full moon doth turn
To swift decay and burn
Her fire away.

One day remembering her kernel-stone
She set it by a wall that faced the south;
Dew'd it with tears, hoped for a root,
Watch'd for a waxing shoot,
But there came none;
It never saw the sun,
It never felt the trickling moisture run:
While with sunk eyes and faded mouth
She dream'd of melons, as a traveller sees
False waves in desert drouth
With shade of leaf-crown'd trees,
And burns the thirstier in the sandful breeze.

She no more swept the house,
Tended the fowls or cows,
Fetch'd honey, kneaded cakes of wheat,
Brought water from the brook:
But sat down listless in the chimney-nook
And would not eat.

Tender Lizzie could not bear
To watch her sister's cankerous care
Yet not to share.

She night and morning
Caught the goblins' cry:
"Come buy our orchard fruits,
Come buy, come buy;"—
Beside the brook, along the glen,
She heard the tramp of goblin men,
The yoke and stir
Poor Laura could not hear;
Long'd to buy fruit to comfort her,
But fear'd to pay too dear.
She thought of Jeanie in her grave,
Who should have been a bride;
But who for joys brides hope to have
Fell sick and died
In her gay prime,
In earliest winter time
With the first glazing rime,
With the first snow-fall of crisp winter time.

Till Laura dwindling
Seem'd knocking at Death's door:
Then Lizzie weigh'd no more
Better and worse;
But put a silver penny in her purse,
Kiss'd Laura, cross'd the heath with clumps of furze
At twilight, halted by the brook:
And for the first time in her life
Began to listen and look.

Laugh'd every goblin
When they spied her peeping:
Came towards her hobbling,
Flying, running, leaping,
Puffing and blowing,
Chuckling, clapping, crowing,
Clucking and gobbling,

Mopping and mowing,
Full of airs and graces,
Pulling wry faces,
Demure grimaces,
Cat-like and rat-like,
Ratel- and wombat-like,
Snail-paced in a hurry,
Parrot-voiced and whistler,
Helter skelter, hurry skurry,
Chattering like magpies,
Fluttering like pigeons,
Gliding like fishes,—
Hugg'd her and kiss'd her:
Squeez'd and caress'd her:
Stretch'd up their dishes,
Panniers, and plates:
"Look at our apples
Russet and dun,
Bob at our cherries,
Bite at our peaches,
Citrons and dates,
Grapes for the asking,
Pears red with basking
Out in the sun,
Plums on their twigs;
Pluck them and suck them,
Pomegranates, figs."—

"Good folk," said Lizzie,
Mindful of Jeanie:
"Give me much and many: —
Held out her apron,
Toss'd them her penny.
"Nay, take a seat with us,
Honour and eat with us,"
They answer'd grinning:

"Our feast is but beginning.
Night yet is early,
Warm and dew-pearly,
Wakeful and starry:
Such fruits as these
No man can carry:
Half their bloom would fly,
Half their dew would dry,
Half their flavour would pass by.
Sit down and feast with us,
Be welcome guest with us,
Cheer you and rest with us."—
"Thank you," said Lizzie: "But one waits
At home alone for me:
So without further parleying,
If you will not sell me any
Of your fruits though much and many,
Give me back my silver penny
I toss'd you for a fee."—
They began to scratch their pates,
No longer wagging, purring,
But visibly demurring,
Grunting and snarling.
One call'd her proud,
Cross-grain'd, uncivil;
Their tones wax'd loud,
Their looks were evil.
Lashing their tails
They trod and hustled her,
Elbow'd and jostled her,
Claw'd with their nails,
Barking, mewing, hissing, mocking,
Tore her gown and soil'd her stocking,
Twitch'd her hair out by the roots,
Stamp'd upon her tender feet,
Held her hands and squeez'd their fruits

Against her mouth to make her eat.

White and golden Lizzie stood,
Like a lily in a flood,—
Like a rock of blue-vein'd stone
Lash'd by tides obstreperously,—
Like a beacon left alone
In a hoary roaring sea,
Sending up a golden fire,—
Like a fruit-crown'd orange-tree
White with blossoms honey-sweet
Sore beset by wasp and bee,—
Like a royal virgin town
Topp'd with gilded dome and spire
Close beleaguer'd by a fleet
Mad to tug her standard down.

One may lead a horse to water,
Twenty cannot make him drink.
Though the goblins cuff'd and caught her,
Coax'd and fought her,
Bullied and besought her,
Scratch'd her, pinch'd her black as ink,
Kick'd and knock'd her,
Maul'd and mock'd her,
Lizzie utter'd not a word;
Would not open lip from lip
Lest they should cram a mouthful in:
But laugh'd in heart to feel the drip
Of juice that syrupp'd all her face,
And lodg'd in dimples of her chin,
And streak'd her neck which quaked like curd.
At last the evil people,
Worn out by her resistance,
Flung back her penny, kick'd their fruit
Along whichever road they took,

Not leaving root or stone or shoot;
Some writh'd into the ground,
Some div'd into the brook
With ring and ripple,
Some scudded on the gale without a sound,
Some vanish'd in the distance.

In a smart, ache, tingle,
Lizzie went her way;
Knew not was it night or day;
Sprang up the bank, tore thro' the furze,
Threaded copse and dingle,
And heard her penny jingle
Bouncing in her purse,—
Its bounce was music to her ear.
She ran and ran
As if she fear'd some goblin man
Dogg'd her with gibe or curse
Or something worse:
But not one goblin scurried after,
Nor was she prick'd by fear;
The kind heart made her windy-paced
That urged her home quite out of breath with haste
And inward laughter.

She cried, "Laura," up the garden,
"Did you miss me?
Come and kiss me.
Never mind my bruises,
Hug me, kiss me, suck my juices
Squeez'd from goblin fruits for you,
Goblin pulp and goblin dew.
Eat me, drink me, love me;
Laura, make much of me;
For your sake I have braved the glen
And had to do with goblin merchant men."

Laura started from her chair,
Flung her arms up in the air,
Clutch'd her hair:
"Lizzie, Lizzie, have you tasted
For my sake the fruit forbidden?
Must your light like mine be hidden,
Your young life like mine be wasted,
Undone in mine undoing,
And ruin'd in my ruin,
Thirsty, canker'd, goblin-ridden?"—
She clung about her sister,
Kiss'd and kiss'd and kiss'd her:
Tears once again
Refresh'd her shrunken eyes,
Dropping like rain
After long sultry drouth;
Shaking with aguish fear, and pain,
She kiss'd and kiss'd her with a hungry mouth.

Her lips began to scorch,
That juice was wormwood to her tongue,
She loath'd the feast:
Writhing as one possess'd she leap'd and sung,
Rent all her robe, and wrung
Her hands in lamentable haste,
And beat her breast.
Her locks stream'd like the torch
Borne by a racer at full speed,
Or like the mane of horses in their flight,
Or like an eagle when she stems the light
Straight toward the sun,
Or like a caged thing freed,
Or like a flying flag when armies run.

Swift fire spread through her veins, knock'd at her heart,

Met the fire smouldering there
And overbore its lesser flame;
She gorged on bitterness without a name:
Ah! fool, to choose such part
Of soul-consuming care!
Sense fail'd in the mortal strife:
Like the watch-tower of a town
Which an earthquake shatters down,
Like a lightning-stricken mast,
Like a wind-uprooted tree
Spun about,
Like a foam-topp'd waterspout
Cast down headlong in the sea,
She fell at last;
Pleasure past and anguish past,
Is it death or is it life?

Life out of death.
That night long Lizzie watch'd by her,
Counted her pulse's flagging stir,
Felt for her breath,
Held water to her lips, and cool'd her face
With tears and fanning leaves:
But when the first birds chirp'd about their eaves,
And early reapers plodded to the place
Of golden sheaves,
And dew-wet grass
Bow'd in the morning winds so brisk to pass,
And new buds with new day
Open'd of cup-like lilies on the stream,
Laura awoke as from a dream,
Laugh'd in the innocent old way,
Hugg'd Lizzie but not twice or thrice;
Her gleaming locks show'd not one thread of grey,
Her breath was sweet as May
And light danced in her eyes.

Days, weeks, months, years
Afterwards, when both were wives
With children of their own;
Their mother-hearts beset with fears,
Their lives bound up in tender lives;
Laura would call the little ones
And tell them of her early prime,
Those pleasant days long gone
Of not-returning time:
Would talk about the haunted glen,
The wicked, quaint fruit-merchant men,
Their fruits like honey to the throat
But poison in the blood;
(Men sell not such in any town):
Would tell them how her sister stood
In deadly peril to do her good,
And win the fiery antidote:
Then joining hands to little hands
Would bid them cling together,
"For there is no friend like a sister
In calm or stormy weather;
To cheer one on the tedious way,
To fetch one if one goes astray,
To lift one if one totters down,
To strengthen whilst one stands."

Bio: On December 5, 1830, Christina Rossetti was born in London, one of four children of Italian parents. Her father was the poet Gabriele Rossetti; her brother Dante Gabriel Rossetti also became a poet and a painter. Rossetti is best known for her ballads and her mystic religious lyrics. Her poetry is marked by symbolism and intense feeling. Rossetti's best-known work, Goblin Market and Other Poems, *was published in 1862. The collection established Rossetti as a significant voice in Victorian poetry. She has been compared to Emily Dickinson but the similarity is*

more in the choice of spiritual topics than in poetic approach, Rossetti's poetry being one of intense feelings, her technique refined within the forms established in her time.

FUNGI FROM YUGGOTH
H.P. Lovecraft

I. The Book

The place was dark and dusty and half-lost
In tangles of old alleys near the quays,
Reeking of strange things brought in from the seas,
And with queer curls of fog that west winds tossed.
Small lozenge panes, obscured by smoke and frost,
Just shewed the books, in piles like twisted trees,
Rotting from floor to roof – congeries
Of crumbling elder lore at little cost.

I entered, charmed, and from a cobwebbed heap
Took up the nearest tome and thumbed it through,
Trembling at curious words that seemed to keep
Some secret, monstrous if one only knew.
Then, looking for some seller old in craft,
I could find nothing but a voice that laughed.

II. Pursuit

I held the book beneath my coat, at pains
To hide the thing from sight in such a place;
Hurrying through the ancient harbor lanes
With often-turning head and nervous pace.
Dull, furtive windows in old tottering brick
Peered at me oddly as I hastened by,
And thinking what they sheltered, I grew sick

For a redeeming glimpse of clean blue sky.

No one had seen me take the thing - but still
A blank laugh echoed in my whirling head,
And I could guess what nighted worlds of ill
Lurked in that volume I had coveted.
The way grew strange - the walls alike and madding -
And far behind me, unseen feet were padding.

III. The Key

I do not know what windings in the waste
Of those strange sea-lanes brought me home once more,
But on my porch I trembled, white with haste
To get inside and bolt the heavy door.
I had the book that told the hidden way
Across the void and through the space-hung screens
That hold the undimensioned worlds at bay,
And keep lost aeons to their own demesnes.

At last the key was mine to those vague visions
Of sunset spires and twilight woods that brood
Dim in the gulfs beyond this earth's precisions,
Lurking as memories of infinitude.
The key was mine, but as I sat there mumbling,
The attic window shook with a faint fumbling.

IV. Recognition

The day had come again, when as a child
I saw - just once - that hollow of old oaks,
Grey with a ground-mist that enfolds and chokes
The slinking shapes which madness has defiled.
It was the same - an herbage rank and wild
Clings round an altar whose carved sign invokes
That Nameless One to whom a thousand smokes

Rose, aeons gone, from unclean towers up-piled.

I saw the body spread on that dank stone,
And knew those things which feasted were not men;
I knew this strange, grey world was not my own,
But Yuggoth, past the starry voids - and then
The body shrieked at me with a dead cry,
And all too late I knew that it was I!

V. Homecoming

The daemon said that he would take me home
To the pale, shadowy land I half recalled
As a high place of stair and terrace, walled
With marble balustrades that sky-winds comb,
While miles below a maze of dome on dome
And tower on tower beside a sea lies sprawled.
Once more, he told me, I would stand enthralled
On those old heights, and hear the far-off foam.

All this he promised, and through sunset's gate
He swept me, past the lapping lakes of flame,
And red-gold thrones of gods without a name
Who shriek in fear at some impending fate.
Then a black gulf with sea-sounds in the night:
'Here was your home,' he mocked, 'when you had sight!'

VI. The Lamp

We found the lamp inside those hollow cliffs
Whose chiseled sign no priest in Thebes could read,
And from whose caverns frightened hieroglyphs
Warned every living creature of earth's breed.
No more was there - just that one brazen bowl
With traces of a curious oil within;
Fretted with some obscurely patterned scroll,

And symbols hinting vaguely of strange sin.

Little the fears of forty centuries meant
To us as we bore off our slender spoil,
And when we scanned it in our darkened tent
We struck a match to test the ancient oil.
It blazed - great God!... But the vast shapes we saw
In that mad flash have seared our lives with awe.

VII. Zaman's Hill

The great hill hung close over the old town,
A precipice against the main street's end;
Green, tall, and wooded, looking darkly down
Upon the steeple at the highway bend.
Two hundred years the whispers had been heard
About what happened on the man-shunned slope -
Tales of an oddly mangled deer or bird,
Or of lost boys whose kin had ceased to hope.

One day the mail-man found no village there,
Nor were its folk or houses seen again;
People came out from Aylesbury to stare -
Yet they all told the mail-man it was plain
That he was mad for saying he had spied
The great hill's gluttonous eyes, and jaws stretched wide.

VIII. The Port

Ten miles from Arkham I had struck the trail
That rides the cliff-edge over Boynton Beach,
And hoped that just at sunset I could reach
The crest that looks on Innsmouth in the vale.
Far out at sea was a retreating sail,
White as hard years of ancient winds could bleach,
But evil with some portent beyond speech,

So that I did not wave my hand or hail.

Sails out of Innsmouth! echoing old renown
Of long-dead times. But now a too-swift night
Is closing in, and I have reached the height
Whence I so often scan the distant town.
The spires and roofs are there - but look! The gloom
Sinks on dark lanes, as lightless as the tomb!

IX. The Courtyard

It was the city I had known before;
The ancient, leprous town where mongrel throngs
Chant to strange gods, and beat unhallowed gongs
In crypts beneath foul alleys near the shore.
The rotting, fish-eyed houses leered at me
From where they leaned, drunk and half-animate,
As edging through the filth I passed the gate
To the black courtyard where the man would be.

The dark walls closed me in, and loud I cursed
That ever I had come to such a den,
When suddenly a score of windows burst
Into wild light, and swarmed with dancing men:
Mad, soundless revels of the dragging dead -
And not a corpse had either hands or head!

X. The Pigeon-Flyers

They took me slumming, where gaunt walls of brick
Bulge outward with a viscous stored-up evil,
And twisted faces, thronging foul and thick,
Wink messages to alien god and devil.
A million fires were blazing in the streets,
And from flat roofs a furtive few would fly
Bedraggled birds into the yawning sky

While hidden drums droned on with measured beats.

I knew those fires were brewing monstrous things,
And that those birds of space had been Outside -
I guessed to what dark planet's crypts they plied,
And what they brought from Thog beneath their wings.
The others laughed - till struck too mute to speak
By what they glimpsed in one bird's evil beak.

XI. The Well

Farmer Seth Atwood was past eighty when
He tried to sink that deep well by his door,
With only Eb to help him bore and bore.
We laughed, and hoped he'd soon be sane again.
And yet, instead, young Eb went crazy, too,
So that they shipped him to the county farm.
Seth bricked the well-mouth up as tight as glue -
Then hacked an artery in his gnarled left arm.

After the funeral we felt bound to get
Out to that well and rip the bricks away,
But all we saw were iron hand-holds set
Down a black hole deeper than we could say.
And yet we put the bricks back - for we found
The hole too deep for any line to sound.

XII. The Howler

They told me not to take the Briggs' Hill path
That used to be the highroad through to Zoar,
For Goody Watkins, hanged in seventeen-four,
Had left a certain monstrous aftermath.
Yet when I disobeyed, and had in view
The vine-hung cottage by the great rock slope,
I could not think of elms or hempen rope,

But wondered why the house still seemed so new.

Stopping a while to watch the fading day,
I heard faint howls, as from a room upstairs,
When through the ivied panes one sunset ray
Struck in, and caught the howler unawares.
I glimpsed - and ran in frenzy from the place,
And from a four-pawed thing with human face.

XIII. Hesperia

The winter sunset, flaming beyond spires
And chimneys half-detached from this dull sphere,
Opens great gates to some forgotten year
Of elder splendours and divine desires.
Expectant wonders burn in those rich fires,
Adventure-fraught, and not untinged with fear;
A row of sphinxes where the way leads clear
Toward walls and turrets quivering to far lyres.

It is the land where beauty's meaning flowers;
Where every unplaced memory has a source;
Where the great river Time begins its course
Down the vast void in starlit streams of hours.
Dreams bring us close - but ancient lore repeats
That human tread has never soiled these streets.

XIV. Star-Winds

It is a certain hour of twilight glooms,
Mostly in autumn, when the star-wind pours
Down hilltop streets, deserted out-of-doors,
But shewing early lamplight from snug rooms.
The dead leaves rush in strange, fantastic twists,
And chimney-smoke whirls round with alien grace,
Heeding geometries of outer space,

While Fomalhaut peers in through southward mists.

This is the hour when moonstruck poets know
What fungi sprout in Yuggoth, and what scents
And tints of flowers fill Nithon's continents,
Such as in no poor earthly garden blow.
Yet for each dream these winds to us convey,
A dozen more of ours they sweep away!

XV. Antarktos

Deep in my dream the great bird whispered queerly
Of the black cone amid the polar waste;
Pushing above the ice-sheet lone and drearly,
By storm-crazed aeons battered and defaced.
Hither no living earth-shapes take their courses,
And only pale auroras and faint suns
Glow on that pitted rock, whose primal sources
Are guessed at dimly by the Elder Ones.

If men should glimpse it, they would merely wonder
What tricky mound of Nature's build they spied;
But the bird told of vaster parts, that under
The mile-deep ice-shroud crouch and brood and bide.
God help the dreamer whose mad visions shew
Those dead eyes set in crystal gulfs below!

XVI. The Window

The house was old, with tangled wings outthrown,
Of which no one could ever half keep track,
And in a small room somewhat near the back
Was an odd window sealed with ancient stone.
There, in a dream-plagued childhood, quite alone
I used to go, where night reigned vague and black;
Parting the cobwebs with a curious lack

Of fear, and with a wonder each time grown.

One later day I brought the masons there
To find what view my dim forbears had shunned,
But as they pierced the stone, a rush of air
Burst from the alien voids that yawned beyond.
They fled - but I peered through and found unrolled
All the wild worlds of which my dreams had told.

XVII. A Memory

There were great steppes, and rocky table-lands
Stretching half-limitless in starlit night,
With alien campfires shedding feeble light
On beasts with tinkling bells, in shaggy bands.
Far to the south the plain sloped low and wide
To a dark zigzag line of wall that lay
Like a huge python of some primal day
Which endless time had chilled and petrified.

I shivered oddly in the cold, thin air,
And wondered where I was and how I came,
When a cloaked form against a campfire's glare
Rose and approached, and called me by my name.
Staring at that dead face beneath the hood,
I ceased to hope - because I understood.

XVIII. The Gardens of Yin

Beyond that wall, whose ancient masonry
Reached almost to the sky in moss-thick towers,
There would be terraced gardens, rich with flowers,
And flutter of bird and butterfly and bee.
There would be walks, and bridges arching over
Warm lotos-pools reflecting temple eaves,
And cherry-trees with delicate boughs and leaves

Against a pink sky where the herons hover.

All would be there, for had not old dreams flung
Open the gate to that stone-lanterned maze
Where drowsy streams spin out their winding ways,
Trailed by green vines from bending branches hung?
I hurried - but when the wall rose, grim and great,
I found there was no longer any gate.

XIX. The Bells

Year after year I heard that faint, far ringing
Of deep-toned bells on the black midnight wind;
Peals from no steeple I could ever find,
But strange, as if across some great void winging.
I searched my dreams and memories for a clue,
And thought of all the chimes my visions carried;
Of quiet Innsmouth, where the white gulls tarried
Around an ancient spire that once I knew.

Always perplexed I heard those far notes falling,
Till one March night the bleak rain splashing cold
Beckoned me back through gateways of recalling
To elder towers where the mad clappers tolled.
They tolled - but from the sunless tides that pour
Through sunken valleys on the sea's dead floor.

XX. Night-Gaunts

Out of what crypt they crawl, I cannot tell,
But every night I see the rubbery things,
Black, horned, and slender, with membraneous wings,
And tails that bear the bifid barb of hell.
They come in legions on the north wind's swell,
With obscene clutch that titillates and stings,
Snatching me off on monstrous voyagings

To grey worlds hidden deep in nightmare's well.

Over the jagged peaks of Thok they sweep,
Heedless of all the cries I try to make,
And down the nether pits to that foul lake
Where the puffed shoggoths splash in doubtful sleep.
But oh! If only they would make some sound,
Or wear a face where faces should be found!

XXI. Nyarlathotep

And at the last from inner Egypt came
The strange dark One to whom the fellahs bowed;
Silent and lean and cryptically proud,
And wrapped in fabrics red as sunset flame.
Throngs pressed around, frantic for his commands,
But leaving, could not tell what they had heard;
While through the nations spread the awestruck word
That wild beasts followed him and licked his hands.

Soon from the sea a noxious birth began;
Forgotten lands with weedy spires of gold;
The ground was cleft, and mad auroras rolled
Down on the quaking citadels of man.
Then, crushing what he chanced to mould in play,
The idiot Chaos blew Earth's dust away.

XXII. Azathoth

Out in the mindless void the daemon bore me,
Past the bright clusters of dimensioned space,
Till neither time nor matter stretched before me,
But only Chaos, without form or place.
Here the vast Lord of All in darkness muttered
Things he had dreamed but could not understand,
While near him shapeless bat-things flopped and fluttered

In idiot vortices that ray-streams fanned.

They danced insanely to the high, thin whining
Of a cracked flute clutched in a monstrous paw,
Whence flow the aimless waves whose chance combining
Gives each frail cosmos its eternal law.
'I am His Messenger,' the daemon said,
As in contempt he struck his Master's head.

XXIII. Mirage

I do not know if ever it existed -
That lost world floating dimly on Time's stream -
And yet I see it often, violet-misted,
And shimmering at the back of some vague dream.
There were strange towers and curious lapping rivers,
Labyrinths of wonder, and low vaults of light,
And bough-crossed skies of flame, like that which quivers
Wistfully just before a winter's night.

Great moors led off to sedgy shores unpeopled,
Where vast birds wheeled, while on a windswept hill
There was a village, ancient and white-steepled,
With evening chimes for which I listen still.
I do not know what land it is - or dare
Ask when or why I was, or will be, there.

XXIV. The Canal

Somewhere in dream there is an evil place
Where tall, deserted buildings crowd along
A deep, black, narrow channel, reeking strong
Of frightful things whence oily currents race.
Lanes with old walls half meeting overhead
Wind off to streets one may or may not know,
And feeble moonlight sheds a spectral glow

Over long rows of windows, dark and dead.

There are no footfalls, and the one soft sound
Is of the oily water as it glides
Under stone bridges, and along the sides
Of its deep flume, to some vague ocean bound.
None lives to tell when that stream washed away
Its dream-lost region from the world of clay.

XXV. St. Toad's

'Beware St. Toad's cracked chimes!' I heard him scream
As I plunged into those mad lanes that wind
In labyrinths obscure and undefined
South of the river where old centuries dream.
He was a furtive figure, bent and ragged,
And in a flash had staggered out of sight,
So still I burrowed onward in the night
Toward where more roof-lines rose, malign and jagged.

No guide-book told of what was lurking here -
But now I heard another old man shriek:
'Beware St.Toad's cracked chimes!' And growing weak,
I paused, when a third greybeard croaked in fear:
'Beware St. Toad's cracked chimes!' Aghast, I fled -
Till suddenly that black spire loomed ahead.

XXVI. The Familiars

John Whateley lived about a mile from town,
Up where the hills begin to huddle thick;
We never thought his wits were very quick,
Seeing the way he let his farm run down.
He used to waste his time on some queer books
He'd found around the attic of his place,
Till funny lines got creased into his face,

And folks all said they didn't like his looks.

When he began those night-howls we declared
He'd better be locked up away from harm,
So three men from the Aylesbury town farm
Went for him - but came back alone and scared.
They'd found him talking to two crouching things
That at their step flew off on great black wings.

XXVII. The Elder Pharos

From Leng, where rocky peaks climb bleak and bare
Under cold stars obscure to human sight,
There shoots at dusk a single beam of light
Whose far blue rays make shepherds whine in prayer.
They say (though none has been there) that it comes
Out of a pharos in a tower of stone,
Where the last Elder One lives on alone,
Talking to Chaos with the beat of drums.

The Thing, they whisper, wears a silken mask
Of yellow, whose queer folds appear to hide
A face not of this earth, though none dares ask
Just what those features are, which bulge inside.
Many, in man's first youth, sought out that glow,
But what they found, no one will ever know.

XXVIII. Expectancy

I cannot tell why some things hold for me
A sense of unplumbed marvels to befall,
Or of a rift in the horizon's wall
Opening to worlds where only gods can be.
There is a breathless, vague expectancy,
As of vast ancient pomps I half recall,
Or wild adventures, uncorporeal,

Ecstasy-fraught, and as a day-dream free.

It is in sunsets and strange city spires,
Old villages and woods and misty downs,
South winds, the sea, low hills, and lighted towns,
Old gardens, half-heard songs, and the moon's fires.
But though its lure alone makes life worth living,
None gains or guesses what it hints at giving.

XXIX. Nostalgia

Once every year, in autumn's wistful glow,
The birds fly out over an ocean waste,
Calling and chattering in a joyous haste
To reach some land their inner memories know.
Great terraced gardens where bright blossoms blow,
And lines of mangoes luscious to the taste,
And temple-groves with branches interlaced
Over cool paths - all these their vague dreams shew.

They search the sea for marks of their old shore -
For the tall city, white and turreted -
But only empty waters stretch ahead,
So that at last they turn away once more.
Yet sunken deep where alien polyps throng,
The old towers miss their lost, remembered song.

XXX. Background

I never can be tied to raw, new things,
For I first saw the light in an old town,
Where from my window huddled roofs sloped down
To a quaint harbour rich with visionings.
Streets with carved doorways where the sunset beams
Flooded old fanlights and small window-panes,
And Georgian steeples topped with gilded vanes -

These were the sights that shaped my childhood dreams.

Such treasures, left from times of cautious leaven,
Cannot but loose the hold of flimsier wraiths
That flit with shifting ways and muddled faiths
Across the changeless walls of earth and heaven.
They cut the moment's thongs and leave me free
To stand alone before eternity.

XXXI. The Dweller

It had been old when Babylon was new;
None knows how long it slept beneath that mound,
Where in the end our questing shovels found
Its granite blocks and brought it back to view.
There were vast pavements and foundation-walls,
And crumbling slabs and statues, carved to shew
Fantastic beings of some long ago
Past anything the world of man recalls.

And then we saw those stone steps leading down
Through a choked gate of graven dolomite
To some black haven of eternal night
Where elder signs and primal secrets frown.
We cleared a path - but raced in mad retreat
When from below we heard those clumping feet.

XXXII. Alienation

His solid flesh had never been away,
For each dawn found him in his usual place,
But every night his spirit loved to race
Through gulfs and worlds remote from common day.
He had seen Yaddith, yet retained his mind,
And come back safely from the Ghooric zone,
When one still night across curved space was thrown

That beckoning piping from the voids behind.

He waked that morning as an older man,
And nothing since has looked the same to him.
Objects around float nebulous and dim -
False, phantom trifles of some vaster plan.
His folk and friends are now an alien throng
To which he struggles vainly to belong.

XXXIII. Harbour Whistles

Over old roofs and past decaying spires
The harbour whistles chant all through the night;
Throats from strange ports, and beaches far and white,
And fabulous oceans, ranged in motley choirs.
Each to the other alien and unknown,
Yet all, by some obscurely focussed force
From brooding gulfs beyond the Zodiac's course,
Fused into one mysterious cosmic drone.

Through shadowy dreams they send a marching line
Of still more shadowy shapes and hints and views;
Echoes from outer voids, and subtle clues
To things which they themselves cannot define.
And always in that chorus, faintly blent,
We catch some notes no earth-ship ever sent.

XXXIV. Recapture

The way led down a dark, half-wooded heath
Where moss-grey boulders humped above the mould,
And curious drops, disquieting and cold,
Sprayed up from unseen streams in gulfs beneath.
There was no wind, nor any trace of sound
In puzzling shrub, or alien-featured tree,
Nor any view before - till suddenly,

Straight in my path, I saw a monstrous mound.

Half to the sky those steep sides loomed upspread,
Rank-grassed, and cluttered by a crumbling flight
Of lava stairs that scaled the fear-topped height
In steps too vast for any human tread.
I shrieked - and knew what primal star and year
Had sucked me back from man's dream-transient sphere!

XXXV. Evening Star

I saw it from that hidden, silent place
Where the old wood half shuts the meadow in.
It shone through all the sunset's glories – thin
At first, but with a slowly brightening face.
Night came, and that lone beacon, amber-hued,
Beat on my sight as never it did of old;
The evening star - but grown a thousandfold
More haunting in this hush and solitude.

It traced strange pictures on the quivering air -
Half-memories that had always filled my eyes -
Vast towers and gardens; curious seas and skies
Of some dim life - I never could tell where.
But now I knew that through the cosmic dome
Those rays were calling from my far, lost home.

XXXVI. Continuity

There is in certain ancient things a trace
Of some dim essence - more than form or weight;
A tenuous aether, indeterminate,
Yet linked with all the laws of time and space.
A faint, veiled sign of continuities
That outward eyes can never quite descry;
Of locked dimensions harbouring years gone by,

And out of reach except for hidden keys.

It moves me most when slanting sunbeams glow
On old farm buildings set against a hill,
And paint with life the shapes which linger still
From centuries less a dream than this we know.
In that strange light I feel I am not far
From the fixt mass whose sides the ages are.

Bio: Howard Phillips Lovecraft, of Providence, Rhode Island, was an American author of horror, fantasy and science fiction. Lovecraft's major inspiration and invention was cosmic horror: life is incomprehensible to human minds and the universe is fundamentally alien. Those who genuinely reason, like his protagonists, gamble with sanity. Lovecraft has developed a cult following for his Cthulhu Mythos, a series of loosely interconnected fictions featuring a pantheon of human-nullifying entities, as well as the Necronomicon, a fictional grimoire of magical rites and forbidden lore. His works were deeply pessimistic and cynical, challenging the values of the Enlightenment, Romanticism and Christianity. Lovecraft's protagonists usually achieve the mirror-opposite of traditional gnosis and mysticism by momentarily glimpsing the horror of ultimate reality. Although Lovecraft's readership was limited during his life, his reputation has grown over the decades. He is now commonly regarded as one of the most influential horror writers of the 20th Century, exerting widespread and indirect influence, and frequently compared to Edgar Allan Poe.

THE LANDING
Matthew Wilson

Miller was first on the surface.
It seemed solid enough to hold his weight.
He didn't hear the creature scream till
it was nearly on him.

Quickly, he lifted his rifle and fired.
The thing howled and fell forward, dead.
Maybe coming here had not been such
a good idea after all.

Miller heard his comrade call from
the shuttle – more of the creatures were
coming. They had weapons, clubs and
fire arms. All had ten fingers.

They held signs bidding death to
the aliens. Miller took the stairs two
at a time and locked the shuttle door. The
conquest of earth would have to wait.

Bio: Matthew Wilson, 30, has had over 100 stories accepted / appearances in such places as Horror Zine, Star*Line, Spellbound, Illumen, James Ward Kirk Publishing, Static Movement, Apokrupha Press, Hazardous Press, Gaslight Press, Sorcerers Signal and many more. He is currently editing his first novel and can be contacted on Twitter @matthew94544267.

THE GREEN HILLS OF EARTH
Robert A. Heinlein

Let the sweet fresh breezes heal me
As they rove around the girth
Of our lovely mother planet
Of the cool, green hills of Earth.

We rot in the moulds of Venus,
We retch at her tainted breath.
Foul are her flooded jungles,
Crawling with unclean death.

[– the harsh bright soil of Luna –
– Saturn's rainbow rings –
– the frozen night of Titan –]

We've tried each spinning space mote
And reckoned its true worth:
Take us back again to the homes of men
On the cool, green hills of Earth.

The arching sky is calling
Spacemen back to their trade.
ALL HANDS! STAND BY! FREE FALLING!
And the lights below us fade.

Out ride the sons of Terra,
Far drives the thundering jet,
Up leaps a race of Earthmen,
Out, far, and onward yet –

We pray for one last landing
On the globe that gave us birth;
Let us rest our eyes on the friendly skies
And the cool, green hills of Earth.

Bio: After leaving the U.S. Navy as a young lieutenant, Robert Anson Heinlein began writing science fiction stories and never looked back. He won four Hugo Awards for best science fiction novel during the 1950s and '60s, earning him the sobriquet of "The Dean of Science Fiction." Stranger in a Strange Land, his 1961 story of an empathetic Mars-born human who comes to live on Earth, is one of the best selling science fiction novels ever. Along with Isaac Asimov and Arthur C. Clarke, Heinlein is considered a father of modern science fiction. His other novels include The Puppet Masters (1951), Double Star (1956, Hugo winner for 1956), Starship Troopers (1959, Hugo winner for 1960), The Moon is a Harsh Mistress (1966, Hugo winner for 1967), Time Enough for Love (1973) and The Number of the Beast (1980).

THE VISITORS
Ed Higgins

They come from the sky
in pairs, mostly.

Wearing invisible moccasins
to hide their tracks.

Or at least because the moccasins
sometimes make them invisible.

But I live alone
and they know that.

So they peer in at the windows
of my bedroom. Sometimes we speak

Through a screen if it is summer.
but I never let them in.

Even though they have faces
innocent as a small child

Their yellow eyes are like cats
or the distant stars I sometimes gaze to.

　　Bio: Ed Higgin's poems and short fiction have appeared in various print and online journals including Star*Line, Untoward Magazine, Short, Fast, and Deadly,

Twisted Tongue Magazine, Danse Macabre, scifakuest, and Planet Magazine, among others. He lives with his wife on a small farm in Yamhill, OR with a menagerie of animals including two whippets, two manx barn cats (who don't care for the whippets), and an alpaca named Machu-Picchu.

LOCKSLEY HALL
Alfred Lord Tennyson

Comrades, leave me here a little, while as yet 'tis early morn;
Leave me here, and when you want me, sound upon the bugle-horn

' Tis the place, and all around it, as of old, the curlews call,
Dreary gleams about the moorland flying over Locksley Hall;

Locksley Hall, that in the distance overlooks the sandy tracts,
And the hollow ocean-ridges roaring into cataracts.

Many a night from yonder ivied casement, ere I went to rest,
Did I look on great Orion sloping slowly to the west.

Many a night I saw the Pleiads, rising thro' the mellow shade,
Glitter like a swarm of fireflies tangled in a silver braid.

Here about the beach I wander'd, nourishing a youth sublime
With the fairy tales of science, and the long result of time;

When the centuries behind me like a fruitful land reposed;
When I clung to all the present for the promise that it closed;

When I dipt into the future far as human eye could see,
Saw the vision of the world and all the wonder that would be.–

In the spring a fuller crimson comes upon the robin's breast;
In the spring the wanton lapwing gets himself another crest;

In the spring a livelier iris changes on the burnish'd dove;
In the spring a young man's fancy lightly turns to thoughts of love.

Then her cheek was pale and thinner than should be for one so young.
And her eyes on all my motions with a mute observance hung.

. . . Love took up the glass of Time, and turn'd it in his glowing hands;
Every moment, lightly shaken, ran itself in golden sands.

Love took up the harp of Life, and smote on all the chords with might;
Smote the chord of Self, that, trembling, past in music out of sight.

Many a morning on the moorland did we hear the copses ring,
And her whisper throng'd my pulses with the fulness of the spring.

Many an evening by the waters did we watch the stately ships,
And our spirits rush'd together at the touching of the lips.

O my cousin, shallow-hearted! O my Amy, mine no more!
O the dreary, dreary moorland! O the barren, barren shore!

Falser than all fancy fathoms, falser than all songs have sung,
Puppet to a father's threat, and servile to a shrewish tongue!

Is it well to wish thee happy?–having known me–to decline
On a range of lower feelings and a narrower heart than mine!

Better thou and I were lying, hidden from the heart's disgrace,
Roll'd in one another's arms, and silent in a last embrace.

Cursed be the social wants that sin against the strength of youth!
Cursed be the social lies that warp us from the living truth!

Cursed be the sickly forms that err from honest Nature's rule!
Cursed be the gold that gilds the straightened forehead of the fool!

. . . I had been content to perish, falling on the foreman's ground,
When the ranks are roll'd in vapour, and the winds are laid with sound.

But the jingling of the guinea helps the hurt that Honor feels,
And the nations do but murmur, snarling at each other's heels.

Can I but relive in sadness? I will turn that earlier page.
Hide me from my deep emotion, O thou wondrous Mother-Age!

Make me feel the wild pulsation that I felt before the strife,
When I heard my days before me, and the tumult of my life;

Yearning for the large excitement that the coming years would yield.
Eager-hearted as a boy when first he leaves his father's field,

And at night along the dusky highway near and nearer drawn,
Sees in heaven the light of London flaring like a dreary dawn;

And his spirit leaps within him to be gone before him then,
Underneath the light he looks at, in among the throngs of men;

Men, my brothers, men the workers, ever reaping something new;
That which they have done but earnest of the things that they shall do.

For I dipt into the future, far as human eye could see,
Saw the Vision of the world, and all the wonder that would be;

Saw the heavens fill with commerce, argosies of magic sails,
Pilots of the purple twilight, dropping down with costly bales;

Heard the heavens fill with shouting, and there rain'd a ghastly dew
From the nations' airy navies grappling in the central blue;

Far along the world-wide whisper of the south-wind rushing warm,
With the standards of the peoples plunging thro' the thunder-storm;

Till the war-drum throbb'd no longer, and the battle-flags were furl'd
In the Parliament of man, the Federation of the world.

There the common sense of most shall hold a fretful realm in awe,
And the kindly earth shall slumber, lapt in universal law.

So I triumph'd ere my passion sweeping thro' me left me dry,
Left me with the palsied hear, and left me with the jaundiced eye;

. . . Yet I doubt not thro' the ages one increasing purpose runs,
And the thoughts of men are widen'd with the process of the suns.

What is that to him that reaps not harvest of his youthful joys,
Tho' the deep heart of existence beat for ever like a boy's?

Knowledge comes, but wisdom lingers, and I linger on the shore,
And the individual withers, and the world is more and more.

Knowledge comes, but with wisdom lingers, and he bears a laden breast,
Full of sad experience, moving toward the stillness of his rest.

Hark, my merry comrades call me, sounding on the bugle-horn,
They to whom my foolish passion were a target for their scorn.

Not in vain the distance beacons. Forward, forward let us range.
Let the great world spin forever down the ringing grooves of change.

Through the shadow of the globe we sweep into the younger day:
Better fifty years of Europe that a cycle of Cathay.

Mother-Age (for mine I knew not) help me as when life begun:
Rift the hills, and roll the waters, flash the lightnings, weigh the Sun.

O, I see the crescent promise of my spirit hath not set.
Ancient founts of inspiration well thro' all my fancy yet.

Howsoever these things be, a long farewell to Locksley Hall!
Now for me the woods may wither, now for me the roof-tree fall.

Comes a vapour from the margin, blackening over heath and holt,
Cramming all the blast before it, in its breast a thunderbolt.

Let it fall on Locksley Hall, with rain or hail, or fire or snow;
For the mighty wind arises, roaring seaward, and I go.

Bio: Alfred Tennyson was born in Somersby, Lincolnshire, the fourth of the twelve children of George Tennyson, clergyman, and his wife, Elizabeth. Tennyson established himself as the most popular poet of the Victorian era. His appearance—a large and bearded man, he regularly wore a cloak and a broad brimmed hat—enhanced his notoriety. He read his poetry with a booming voice, often compared to that of Dylan Thomas. In 1859, Tennyson published the first poems of Idylls of the Kings, which sold more than 10,000 copies in one month. In 1884, he accepted a peerage, becoming Alfred Lord Tennyson.

THE STARS ARE CALLING
Mathias Jansson

A distant beacon
a pulsating dark hole
echoing with a message
from the beginning of time

Unveiled dimensions leaking
information into time and space
traveling beyond the speed of light

In the deep caves of the desert
the still surface with water
ripples with meaning
detectors revealing
horrifying news

Scientists stare at blank monitors
when suddenly it happens
a message appears
a warning flashing on the screens

Beware, a dangerous species escaping
from the laboratory of Eden
spreading as a disease
killing all the life in Universe.

Bio: Mathias Jansson is a Swedish art critic and horror poet. He has been

published in magazines as The Horror Zine Magazine, Dark Eclipse, Schlock, The Sirens Call, Apehlion and Trembles Horror Magazine. He has also contributed to several anthologies from Horrified Press, James Ward Kirk Fiction, Source Point Press and other publisher. Homepage: http://mathiasjansson72.blogspot.se/.

DISCOMBOBULATION
Rami Sebai

Professor Podluck's macro-biotic,
discombobulating, decollated, self-perpetuating
stereoscopic, spirographical, self-cleaning
modulated, cognitive barista machine
for spatial diagnostic, calculation and time travel.

SHADOW OF DREAMS
Robert E. Howard

Stay not from me that veil of dreams that gives
Strange seas and and skies and lands and curious fire,
Black dragons, crimson moons and white desire,
That through the silvery fabric sifts and sieves
Strange shadows, shades and all unmeasured things,
And in the sifting lends them shapes and wings
And makes them known in ways past common knowing–
Red lands, black seas and ivory rivers flowing.

How of the gold we gather in our hands?
It cheers, but shall escape us at the last,
And shall mean less, when this brief day is past,
Than that we gathered on the yellow sands,
The phantom ore we found in Wizard-lands.

Keep not from me my veil of curious dreams
Through which I see the giant things which drink
From mountain-castled rivers–on the brink
Black elephants that woo the fronded streams,
And golden tom-toms pulsing through the dusk,
And yellow stars, black trees and red-eyed cats,
And bales of silk and amber jars of musk,
And opal shrines and tents and vampire bats.

Long highways climbing eastward to the moon,
And caravans of camels lade with spice,
And ancient sword hilts carved with scroll and rune,
And marble queens with eyes of crimson ice.

Uncharted shores where moons of scarlet spray
Break on a Viking's galley on the sand,
And curtains held by one slim silver band
That float from casements opening on a bay,
And monstrous iron castles, dragon-barred,
And purple cloaks with inlaid gems bestarred.

Long silver tasseled mantles, curious furs,
And camel bells and dawns and golden heat,
And tuneful rattle of the horseman's spurs
Along some sleeping desert city's street.

Time strides and all too soon shall I grow old
With still all earth to see, all life to live:
Then come to me, my silver veil, and sieve,
Seas of illusion beached with magic gold.

Bio: Robert Ervin Howard was an extraordinarily prolific and inventive writer of fiction and poetry during the 1920s and 1930s. Although best known as the creator of Conan, REH wrote hundreds of poems and over three hundred works of fiction in a wide range of genres – about half of which were published during his tragically short career. REH's unique synthesis of historical adventure, fantasy, and horror created what we now known as sword and sorcery.

ARMAGEDDON
M.A. Crawford

She said,
"I wanted to see the end of the universe."
And I said,
"You can't, because it hasn't happened yet."
She said,
"Don't be smart."

And I thought about that–
and then the stars,
and the way light travels
through the universe,
even when they have
lost their glow,
and then how
it all ends,
and when we end,
and if we do
it won't be over
because
we will
still be
light
traveling
and matter–
floating.

THE HOSTING OF THE SIDHE
William Butler Yeats

The host is riding from Knocknarea
And over the grave of Clooth-na-Bare;
Caoilte tossing his burning hair,
And Niamh calling Away, come away:
Empty your heart of its mortal dream.
The winds awaken, the leaves whirl round,
Our cheeks are pale, our hair is unbound,
Our breasts are heaving our eyes are agleam,
Our arms are waving our lips are apart;
And if any gaze on our rushing band,
We come between him and the deed of his hand,
We come between him and the hope of his heart.
The host is rushing 'twixt night and day,
And where is there hope or deed as fair?
Caoilte tossing his burning hair,
And Niamh calling Away, come away.

Bio: William Butler Yeats was an Irish poet and one of the foremost figures of 20th century literature. A pillar of both the Irish and British literary establishments, in his later years he served as an Irish Senator for two terms.

THE CENTAURS
Rudyard Kipling

Up came the young Centaur-colts from the plains they were
  fathered in–
  Curious, awkward, afraid.
Burrs on their hocks and their tails, they were branded and gath-
  ered in
  Mobs and run up to the yard to be made.

Starting and shying at straws, with sidlings and plungings,
  Buckings and whirlings and bolts;
Greener than grass, but full-ripe for their bridling and lungings,
  Up to the yards and to Chiron they bustled the colts...

First the light web and the cavesson; then the linked keys
  To jingle and turn on the tongue. Then, with cocked ears,
The hours of watching and envy, while comrades at ease
  Passaged and backed, making naught of these terrible gears.

Next, over-pride and its price at the low-seeming fence
  Too oft and too easily taken – the world-beheld fall!
And none in the yard except Chiron to doubt the immense,
  Irretrievable shame of it all!...

Last, the trained squadron, full-charge–the sound of a going
  Through dust and spun clods, and strong kicks, pelted in as
    they went,
And repaid at top-speed; till the order to halt without slowing
  Showed every colt on his haunches–and Chiron content!

Bio: Joseph Rudyard Kipling was an English short-story writer, poet, and novelist. He wrote tales and poems of British soldiers in India and stories for children.

LAMIA
John Keats

I.

Upon a time, before the faery broods
Drove Nymph and Satyr from the prosperous woods,
Before King Oberon's bright diadem,
Sceptre, and mantle, clasp'd with dewy gem,
Frighted away the Dryads and the Fauns
From rushes green, and brakes, and cowslip'd lawns,
The ever-smitten Hermes empty left
His golden throne, bent warm on amorous theft:
From high Olympus had he stolen light,
On this side of Jove's clouds, to escape the sight
Of his great summoner, and made retreat
Into a forest on the shores of Crete.
For somewhere in that sacred island dwelt
A nymph, to whom all hoofed Satyrs knelt;
At whose white feet the languid Tritons poured
Pearls, while on land they wither'd and adored.
Fast by the springs where she to bathe was wont,
And in those meads where sometime she might haunt,
Were strewn rich gifts, unknown to any Muse,
Though Fancy's casket were unlock'd to choose.
Ah, what a world of love was at her feet!
So Hermes thought, and a celestial heat
Burnt from his winged heels to either ear,
That from a whiteness, as the lily clear,
Blush'd into roses 'mid his golden hair,
Fallen in jealous curls about his shoulders bare.
From vale to vale, from wood to wood, he flew,

Breathing upon the flowers his passion new,
And wound with many a river to its head,
To find where this sweet nymph prepar'd her secret bed:
In vain; the sweet nymph might nowhere be found,
And so he rested, on the lonely ground,
Pensive, and full of painful jealousies
Of the Wood-Gods, and even the very trees.
There as he stood, he heard a mournful voice,
Such as once heard, in gentle heart, destroys
All pain but pity: thus the lone voice spake:
"When from this wreathed tomb shall I awake!
When move in a sweet body fit for life,
And love, and pleasure, and the ruddy strife
Of hearts and lips! Ah, miserable me!"
The God, dove-footed, glided silently
Round bush and tree, soft-brushing, in his speed,
The taller grasses and full-flowering weed,
Until he found a palpitating snake,
Bright, and cirque-couchant in a dusky brake.

She was a gordian shape of dazzling hue,
Vermilion-spotted, golden, green, and blue;
Striped like a zebra, freckled like a pard,
Eyed like a peacock, and all crimson barr'd;
And full of silver moons, that, as she breathed,
Dissolv'd, or brighter shone, or interwreathed
Their lustres with the gloomier tapestries -
So rainbow-sided, touch'd with miseries,
She seem'd, at once, some penanced lady elf,
Some demon's mistress, or the demon's self.
Upon her crest she wore a wannish fire
Sprinkled with stars, like Ariadne's tiar:
Her head was serpent, but ah, bitter-sweet!
She had a woman's mouth with all its pearls complete:
And for her eyes: what could such eyes do there
But weep, and weep, that they were born so fair?

As Proserpine still weeps for her Sicilian air.
Her throat was serpent, but the words she spake
Came, as through bubbling honey, for Love's sake,
And thus; while Hermes on his pinions lay,
Like a stoop'd falcon ere he takes his prey.

"Fair Hermes, crown'd with feathers, fluttering light,
I had a splendid dream of thee last night:
I saw thee sitting, on a throne of gold,
Among the Gods, upon Olympus old,
The only sad one; for thou didst not hear
The soft, lute-finger'd Muses chaunting clear,
Nor even Apollo when he sang alone,
Deaf to his throbbing throat's long, long melodious moan.
I dreamt I saw thee, robed in purple flakes,
Break amorous through the clouds, as morning breaks,
And, swiftly as a bright Phoebean dart,
Strike for the Cretan isle; and here thou art!
Too gentle Hermes, hast thou found the maid?"
Whereat the star of Lethe not delay'd
His rosy eloquence, and thus inquired:
"Thou smooth-lipp'd serpent, surely high inspired!
Thou beauteous wreath, with melancholy eyes,
Possess whatever bliss thou canst devise,
Telling me only where my nymph is fled, -
Where she doth breathe!" "Bright planet, thou hast said,"
Return'd the snake, "but seal with oaths, fair God!"
"I swear," said Hermes, "by my serpent rod,
And by thine eyes, and by thy starry crown!"
Light flew his earnest words, among the blossoms blown.
Then thus again the brilliance feminine:
"Too frail of heart! for this lost nymph of thine,
Free as the air, invisibly, she strays
About these thornless wilds; her pleasant days
She tastes unseen; unseen her nimble feet
Leave traces in the grass and flowers sweet;

From weary tendrils, and bow'd branches green,
She plucks the fruit unseen, she bathes unseen:
And by my power is her beauty veil'd
To keep it unaffronted, unassail'd
By the love-glances of unlovely eyes,
Of Satyrs, Fauns, and blear'd Silenus' sighs.
Pale grew her immortality, for woe
Of all these lovers, and she grieved so
I took compassion on her, bade her steep
Her hair in weird syrops, that would keep
Her loveliness invisible, yet free
To wander as she loves, in liberty.
Thou shalt behold her, Hermes, thou alone,
If thou wilt, as thou swearest, grant my boon!"
Then, once again, the charmed God began
An oath, and through the serpent's ears it ran
Warm, tremulous, devout, psalterian.
Ravish'd, she lifted her Circean head,
Blush'd a live damask, and swift-lisping said,
"I was a woman, let me have once more
A woman's shape, and charming as before.
I love a youth of Corinth - O the bliss!
Give me my woman's form, and place me where he is.
Stoop, Hermes, let me breathe upon thy brow,
And thou shalt see thy sweet nymph even now."
The God on half-shut feathers sank serene,
She breath'd upon his eyes, and swift was seen
Of both the guarded nymph near-smiling on the green.
It was no dream; or say a dream it was,
Real are the dreams of Gods, and smoothly pass
Their pleasures in a long immortal dream.
One warm, flush'd moment, hovering, it might seem
Dash'd by the wood-nymph's beauty, so he burn'd;
Then, lighting on the printless verdure, turn'd
To the swoon'd serpent, and with languid arm,
Delicate, put to proof the lythe Caducean charm.

So done, upon the nymph his eyes he bent,
Full of adoring tears and blandishment,
And towards her stept: she, like a moon in wane,
Faded before him, cower'd, nor could restrain
Her fearful sobs, self-folding like a flower
That faints into itself at evening hour:
But the God fostering her chilled hand,
She felt the warmth, her eyelids open'd bland,
And, like new flowers at morning song of bees,
Bloom'd, and gave up her honey to the lees.
Into the green-recessed woods they flew;
Nor grew they pale, as mortal lovers do.

Left to herself, the serpent now began
To change; her elfin blood in madness ran,
Her mouth foam'd, and the grass, therewith besprent,
Wither'd at dew so sweet and virulent;
Her eyes in torture fix'd, and anguish drear,
Hot, glaz'd, and wide, with lid-lashes all sear,
Flash'd phosphor and sharp sparks, without one cooling tear.
The colours all inflam'd throughout her train,
She writh'd about, convuls'd with scarlet pain:
A deep volcanian yellow took the place
Of all her milder-mooned body's grace;
And, as the lava ravishes the mead,
Spoilt all her silver mail, and golden brede;
Made gloom of all her frecklings, streaks and bars,
Eclips'd her crescents, and lick'd up her stars:
So that, in moments few, she was undrest
Of all her sapphires, greens, and amethyst,
And rubious-argent: of all these bereft,
Nothing but pain and ugliness were left.
Still shone her crown; that vanish'd, also she
Melted and disappear'd as suddenly;
And in the air, her new voice luting soft,
Cried, "Lycius! gentle Lycius!" - Borne aloft

With the bright mists about the mountains hoar
These words dissolv'd: Crete's forests heard no more.

Whither fled Lamia, now a lady bright,
A full-born beauty new and exquisite?
She fled into that valley they pass o'er
Who go to Corinth from Cenchreas' shore;
And rested at the foot of those wild hills,
The rugged founts of the Peraean rills,
And of that other ridge whose barren back
Stretches, with all its mist and cloudy rack,
South-westward to Cleone. There she stood
About a young bird's flutter from a wood,
Fair, on a sloping green of mossy tread,
By a clear pool, wherein she passioned
To see herself escap'd from so sore ills,
While her robes flaunted with the daffodils.

Ah, happy Lycius! - for she was a maid
More beautiful than ever twisted braid,
Or sigh'd, or blush'd, or on spring-flowered lea
Spread a green kirtle to the minstrelsy:
A virgin purest lipp'd, yet in the lore
Of love deep learned to the red heart's core:
Not one hour old, yet of sciential brain
To unperplex bliss from its neighbour pain;
Define their pettish limits, and estrange
Their points of contact, and swift counterchange;
Intrigue with the specious chaos, and dispart
Its most ambiguous atoms with sure art;
As though in Cupid's college she had spent
Sweet days a lovely graduate, still unshent,
And kept his rosy terms in idle languishment.

Why this fair creature chose so fairily
By the wayside to linger, we shall see;

But first 'tis fit to tell how she could muse
And dream, when in the serpent prison-house,
Of all she list, strange or magnificent:
How, ever, where she will'd, her spirit went;
Whether to faint Elysium, or where
Down through tress-lifting waves the Nereids fair
Wind into Thetis' bower by many a pearly stair;
Or where God Bacchus drains his cups divine,
Stretch'd out, at ease, beneath a glutinous pine;
Or where in Pluto's gardens palatine
Mulciber's columns gleam in far piazzian line.
And sometimes into cities she would send
Her dream, with feast and rioting to blend;
And once, while among mortals dreaming thus,
She saw the young Corinthian Lycius
Charioting foremost in the envious race,
Like a young Jove with calm uneager face,
And fell into a swooning love of him.
Now on the moth-time of that evening dim
He would return that way, as well she knew,
To Corinth from the shore; for freshly blew
The eastern soft wind, and his galley now
Grated the quaystones with her brazen prow
In port Cenchreas, from Egina isle
Fresh anchor'd; whither he had been awhile
To sacrifice to Jove, whose temple there
Waits with high marble doors for blood and incense rare.
Jove heard his vows, and better'd his desire;
For by some freakful chance he made retire
From his companions, and set forth to walk,
Perhaps grown wearied of their Corinth talk:
Over the solitary hills he fared,
Thoughtless at first, but ere eve's star appeared
His phantasy was lost, where reason fades,
In the calm'd twilight of Platonic shades.
Lamia beheld him coming, near, more near -

Close to her passing, in indifference drear,
His silent sandals swept the mossy green;
So neighbour'd to him, and yet so unseen
She stood: he pass'd, shut up in mysteries,
His mind wrapp'd like his mantle, while her eyes
Follow'd his steps, and her neck regal white
Turn'd - syllabling thus, "Ah, Lycius bright,
And will you leave me on the hills alone?
Lycius, look back! and be some pity shown."
He did; not with cold wonder fearingly,
But Orpheus-like at an Eurydice;
For so delicious were the words she sung,
It seem'd he had lov'd them a whole summer long:
And soon his eyes had drunk her beauty up,
Leaving no drop in the bewildering cup,
And still the cup was full, - while he afraid
Lest she should vanish ere his lip had paid
Due adoration, thus began to adore;
Her soft look growing coy, she saw his chain so sure:
"Leave thee alone! Look back! Ah, Goddess, see
Whether my eyes can ever turn from thee!
For pity do not this sad heart belie -
Even as thou vanishest so I shall die.
Stay! though a Naiad of the rivers, stay!
To thy far wishes will thy streams obey:
Stay! though the greenest woods be thy domain,
Alone they can drink up the morning rain:
Though a descended Pleiad, will not one
Of thine harmonious sisters keep in tune
Thy spheres, and as thy silver proxy shine?
So sweetly to these ravish'd ears of mine
Came thy sweet greeting, that if thou shouldst fade
Thy memory will waste me to a shade -
For pity do not melt!" - "If I should stay,"
Said Lamia, "here, upon this floor of clay,
And pain my steps upon these flowers too rough,

What canst thou say or do of charm enough
To dull the nice remembrance of my home?
Thou canst not ask me with thee here to roam
Over these hills and vales, where no joy is, -
Empty of immortality and bliss!
Thou art a scholar, Lycius, and must know
That finer spirits cannot breathe below
In human climes, and live: Alas! poor youth,
What taste of purer air hast thou to soothe
My essence? What serener palaces,
Where I may all my many senses please,
And by mysterious sleights a hundred thirsts appease?
It cannot be - Adieu!" So said, she rose
Tiptoe with white arms spread. He, sick to lose
The amorous promise of her lone complain,
Swoon'd, murmuring of love, and pale with pain.
The cruel lady, without any show
Of sorrow for her tender favourite's woe,
But rather, if her eyes could brighter be,
With brighter eyes and slow amenity,
Put her new lips to his, and gave afresh
The life she had so tangled in her mesh:
And as he from one trance was wakening
Into another, she began to sing,
Happy in beauty, life, and love, and every thing,
A song of love, too sweet for earthly lyres,
While, like held breath, the stars drew in their panting fires
And then she whisper'd in such trembling tone,
As those who, safe together met alone
For the first time through many anguish'd days,
Use other speech than looks; bidding him raise
His drooping head, and clear his soul of doubt,
For that she was a woman, and without
Any more subtle fluid in her veins
Than throbbing blood, and that the self-same pains
Inhabited her frail-strung heart as his.

And next she wonder'd how his eyes could miss
Her face so long in Corinth, where, she said,
She dwelt but half retir'd, and there had led
Days happy as the gold coin could invent
Without the aid of love; yet in content
Till she saw him, as once she pass'd him by,
Where 'gainst a column he leant thoughtfully
At Venus' temple porch, 'mid baskets heap'd
Of amorous herbs and flowers, newly reap'd
Late on that eve, as 'twas the night before
The Adonian feast; whereof she saw no more,
But wept alone those days, for why should she adore?
Lycius from death awoke into amaze,
To see her still, and singing so sweet lays;
Then from amaze into delight he fell
To hear her whisper woman's lore so well;
And every word she spake entic'd him on
To unperplex'd delight and pleasure known.
Let the mad poets say whate'er they please
Of the sweets of Fairies, Peris, Goddesses,
There is not such a treat among them all,
Haunters of cavern, lake, and waterfall,
As a real woman, lineal indeed
From Pyrrha's pebbles or old Adam's seed.
Thus gentle Lamia judg'd, and judg'd aright,
That Lycius could not love in half a fright,
So threw the goddess off, and won his heart
More pleasantly by playing woman's part,
With no more awe than what her beauty gave,
That, while it smote, still guaranteed to save.
Lycius to all made eloquent reply,
Marrying to every word a twinborn sigh;
And last, pointing to Corinth, ask'd her sweet,
If 'twas too far that night for her soft feet.
The way was short, for Lamia's eagerness
Made, by a spell, the triple league decrease

To a few paces; not at all surmised
By blinded Lycius, so in her comprized.
They pass'd the city gates, he knew not how
So noiseless, and he never thought to know.

As men talk in a dream, so Corinth all,
Throughout her palaces imperial,
And all her populous streets and temples lewd,
Mutter'd, like tempest in the distance brew'd,
To the wide-spreaded night above her towers.
Men, women, rich and poor, in the cool hours,
Shuffled their sandals o'er the pavement white,
Companion'd or alone; while many a light
Flared, here and there, from wealthy festivals,
And threw their moving shadows on the walls,
Or found them cluster'd in the corniced shade
Of some arch'd temple door, or dusky colonnade.

Muffling his face, of greeting friends in fear,
Her fingers he press'd hard, as one came near
With curl'd gray beard, sharp eyes, and smooth bald crown,
Slow-stepp'd, and robed in philosophic gown:
Lycius shrank closer, as they met and past,
Into his mantle, adding wings to haste,
While hurried Lamia trembled: "Ah," said he,
"Why do you shudder, love, so ruefully?
Why does your tender palm dissolve in dew?" -
"I'm wearied," said fair Lamia: "tell me who
Is that old man? I cannot bring to mind
His features - Lycius! wherefore did you blind
Yourself from his quick eyes?" Lycius replied,
'Tis Apollonius sage, my trusty guide
And good instructor; but to-night he seems
The ghost of folly haunting my sweet dreams.

While yet he spake they had arrived before

A pillar'd porch, with lofty portal door,
Where hung a silver lamp, whose phosphor glow
Reflected in the slabbed steps below,
Mild as a star in water; for so new,
And so unsullied was the marble hue,
So through the crystal polish, liquid fine,
Ran the dark veins, that none but feet divine
Could e'er have touch'd there. Sounds Aeolian
Breath'd from the hinges, as the ample span
Of the wide doors disclos'd a place unknown
Some time to any, but those two alone,
And a few Persian mutes, who that same year
Were seen about the markets: none knew where
They could inhabit; the most curious
Were foil'd, who watch'd to trace them to their house:
And but the flitter-winged verse must tell,
For truth's sake, what woe afterwards befel,
'Twould humour many a heart to leave them thus,
Shut from the busy world of more incredulous.

II.

love in a hut, with water and a crust,
Is - Love, forgive us! - cinders, ashes, dust;
Love in a palace is perhaps at last
More grievous torment than a hermit's fast -
That is a doubtful tale from faery land,
Hard for the non-elect to understand.
Had Lycius liv'd to hand his story down,
He might have given the moral a fresh frown,
Or clench'd it quite: but too short was their bliss
To breed distrust and hate, that make the soft voice hiss.
Besides, there, nightly, with terrific glare,
Love, jealous grown of so complete a pair,
Hover'd and buzz'd his wings, with fearful roar,
Above the lintel of their chamber door,

And down the passage cast a glow upon the floor.

For all this came a ruin: side by side
They were enthroned, in the even tide,
Upon a couch, near to a curtaining
Whose airy texture, from a golden string,
Floated into the room, and let appear
Unveil'd the summer heaven, blue and clear,
Betwixt two marble shafts: - there they reposed,
Where use had made it sweet, with eyelids closed,
Saving a tythe which love still open kept,
That they might see each other while they almost slept;
When from the slope side of a suburb hill,
Deafening the swallow's twitter, came a thrill
Of trumpets - Lycius started - the sounds fled,
But left a thought, a buzzing in his head.
For the first time, since first he harbour'd in
That purple-lined palace of sweet sin,
His spirit pass'd beyond its golden bourn
Into the noisy world almost forsworn.
The lady, ever watchful, penetrant,
Saw this with pain, so arguing a want
Of something more, more than her empery
Of joys; and she began to moan and sigh
Because he mused beyond her, knowing well
That but a moment's thought is passion's passing bell.
"Why do you sigh, fair creature?" whisper'd he:
"Why do you think?" return'd she tenderly:
"You have deserted me - where am I now?
Not in your heart while care weighs on your brow:
No, no, you have dismiss'd me; and I go
From your breast houseless: ay, it must be so."
He answer'd, bending to her open eyes,
Where he was mirror'd small in paradise,
My silver planet, both of eve and morn!
Why will you plead yourself so sad forlorn,

While I am striving how to fill my heart
With deeper crimson, and a double smart?
How to entangle, trammel up and snare
Your soul in mine, and labyrinth you there
Like the hid scent in an unbudded rose?
Ay, a sweet kiss - you see your mighty woes.
My thoughts! shall I unveil them? Listen then!
What mortal hath a prize, that other men
May be confounded and abash'd withal,
But lets it sometimes pace abroad majestical,
And triumph, as in thee I should rejoice
Amid the hoarse alarm of Corinth's voice.
Let my foes choke, and my friends shout afar,
While through the thronged streets your bridal car
Wheels round its dazzling spokes." The lady's cheek
Trembled; she nothing said, but, pale and meek,
Arose and knelt before him, wept a rain
Of sorrows at his words; at last with pain
Beseeching him, the while his hand she wrung,
To change his purpose. He thereat was stung,
Perverse, with stronger fancy to reclaim
Her wild and timid nature to his aim:
Besides, for all his love, in self despite,
Against his better self, he took delight
Luxurious in her sorrows, soft and new.
His passion, cruel grown, took on a hue
Fierce and sanguineous as 'twas possible
In one whose brow had no dark veins to swell.
Fine was the mitigated fury, like
Apollo's presence when in act to strike
The serpent - Ha, the serpent! certes, she
Was none. She burnt, she lov'd the tyranny,
And, all subdued, consented to the hour
When to the bridal he should lead his paramour.
Whispering in midnight silence, said the youth,
"Sure some sweet name thou hast, though, by my truth,

I have not ask'd it, ever thinking thee
Not mortal, but of heavenly progeny,
As still I do. Hast any mortal name,
Fit appellation for this dazzling frame?
Or friends or kinsfolk on the citied earth,
To share our marriage feast and nuptial mirth?"
"I have no friends," said Lamia," no, not one;
My presence in wide Corinth hardly known:
My parents' bones are in their dusty urns
Sepulchred, where no kindled incense burns,
Seeing all their luckless race are dead, save me,
And I neglect the holy rite for thee.
Even as you list invite your many guests;
But if, as now it seems, your vision rests
With any pleasure on me, do not bid
Old Apollonius - from him keep me hid."
Lycius, perplex'd at words so blind and blank,
Made close inquiry; from whose touch she shrank,
Feigning a sleep; and he to the dull shade
Of deep sleep in a moment was betray'd

It was the custom then to bring away
The bride from home at blushing shut of day,
Veil'd, in a chariot, heralded along
By strewn flowers, torches, and a marriage song,
With other pageants: but this fair unknown
Had not a friend. So being left alone,
(Lycius was gone to summon all his kin)
And knowing surely she could never win
His foolish heart from its mad pompousness,
She set herself, high-thoughted, how to dress
The misery in fit magnificence.
She did so, but 'tis doubtful how and whence
Came, and who were her subtle servitors.
About the halls, and to and from the doors,
There was a noise of wings, till in short space

The glowing banquet-room shone with wide-arched grace.
A haunting music, sole perhaps and lone
Supportress of the faery-roof, made moan
Throughout, as fearful the whole charm might fade.
Fresh carved cedar, mimicking a glade
Of palm and plantain, met from either side,
High in the midst, in honour of the bride:
Two palms and then two plantains, and so on,
From either side their stems branch'd one to one
All down the aisled place; and beneath all
There ran a stream of lamps straight on from wall to wall.
So canopied, lay an untasted feast
Teeming with odours. Lamia, regal drest,
Silently paced about, and as she went,
In pale contented sort of discontent,
Mission'd her viewless servants to enrich
The fretted splendour of each nook and niche.
Between the tree-stems, marbled plain at first,
Came jasper pannels; then, anon, there burst
Forth creeping imagery of slighter trees,
And with the larger wove in small intricacies.
Approving all, she faded at self-will,
And shut the chamber up, close, hush'd and still,
Complete and ready for the revels rude,
When dreadful guests would come to spoil her solitude.

The day appear'd, and all the gossip rout.
O senseless Lycius! Madman! wherefore flout
The silent-blessing fate, warm cloister'd hours,
And show to common eyes these secret bowers?
The herd approach'd; each guest, with busy brain,
Arriving at the portal, gaz'd amain,
And enter'd marveling: for they knew the street,
Remember'd it from childhood all complete
Without a gap, yet ne'er before had seen
That royal porch, that high-built fair demesne;

So in they hurried all, maz'd, curious and keen:
Save one, who look'd thereon with eye severe,
And with calm-planted steps walk'd in austere;
'Twas Apollonius: something too he laugh'd,
As though some knotty problem, that had daft
His patient thought, had now begun to thaw,
And solve and melt - 'twas just as he foresaw.

He met within the murmurous vestibule
His young disciple. "'Tis no common rule,
Lycius," said he, "for uninvited guest
To force himself upon you, and infest
With an unbidden presence the bright throng
Of younger friends; yet must I do this wrong,
And you forgive me." Lycius blush'd, and led
The old man through the inner doors broad-spread;
With reconciling words and courteous mien
Turning into sweet milk the sophist's spleen.

Of wealthy lustre was the banquet-room,
Fill'd with pervading brilliance and perfume:
Before each lucid pannel fuming stood
A censer fed with myrrh and spiced wood,
Each by a sacred tripod held aloft,
Whose slender feet wide-swerv'd upon the soft
Wool-woofed carpets: fifty wreaths of smoke
From fifty censers their light voyage took
To the high roof, still mimick'd as they rose
Along the mirror'd walls by twin-clouds odorous.
Twelve sphered tables, by silk seats insphered,
High as the level of a man's breast rear'd
On libbard's paws, upheld the heavy gold
Of cups and goblets, and the store thrice told
Of Ceres' horn, and, in huge vessels, wine
Come from the gloomy tun with merry shine.
Thus loaded with a feast the tables stood,

Each shrining in the midst the image of a God.

When in an antichamber every guest
Had felt the cold full sponge to pleasure press'd,
By minist'ring slaves, upon his hands and feet,
And fragrant oils with ceremony meet
Pour'd on his hair, they all mov'd to the feast
In white robes, and themselves in order placed
Around the silken couches, wondering
Whence all this mighty cost and blaze of wealth could spring.

Soft went the music the soft air along,
While fluent Greek a vowel'd undersong
Kept up among the guests discoursing low
At first, for scarcely was the wine at flow;
But when the happy vintage touch'd their brains,
Louder they talk, and louder come the strains
Of powerful instruments - the gorgeous dyes,
The space, the splendour of the draperies,
The roof of awful richness, nectarous cheer,
Beautiful slaves, and Lamia's self, appear,
Now, when the wine has done its rosy deed,
And every soul from human trammels freed,
No more so strange; for merry wine, sweet wine,
Will make Elysian shades not too fair, too divine.
Soon was God Bacchus at meridian height;
Flush'd were their cheeks, and bright eyes double bright:
Garlands of every green, and every scent
From vales deflower'd, or forest-trees branch rent,
In baskets of bright osier'd gold were brought
High as the handles heap'd, to suit the thought
Of every guest; that each, as he did please,
Might fancy-fit his brows, silk-pillow'd at his ease.

What wreath for Lamia? What for Lycius?
What for the sage, old Apollonius?

Upon her aching forehead be there hung
The leaves of willow and of adder's tongue;
And for the youth, quick, let us strip for him
The thyrsus, that his watching eyes may swim
Into forgetfulness; and, for the sage,
Let spear-grass and the spiteful thistle wage
War on his temples. Do not all charms fly
At the mere touch of cold philosophy?
There was an awful rainbow once in heaven:
We know her woof, her texture; she is given
In the dull catalogue of common things.
Philosophy will clip an Angel's wings,
Conquer all mysteries by rule and line,
Empty the haunted air, and gnomed mine -
Unweave a rainbow, as it erewhile made
The tender-person'd Lamia melt into a shade.

By her glad Lycius sitting, in chief place,
Scarce saw in all the room another face,
Till, checking his love trance, a cup he took
Full brimm'd, and opposite sent forth a look
'Cross the broad table, to beseech a glance
From his old teacher's wrinkled countenance,
And pledge him. The bald-head philosopher
Had fix'd his eye, without a twinkle or stir
Full on the alarmed beauty of the bride,
Brow-beating her fair form, and troubling her sweet pride.
Lycius then press'd her hand, with devout touch,
As pale it lay upon the rosy couch:
'Twas icy, and the cold ran through his veins;
Then sudden it grew hot, and all the pains
Of an unnatural heat shot to his heart.
"Lamia, what means this? Wherefore dost thou start?
Know'st thou that man?" Poor Lamia answer'd not.
He gaz'd into her eyes, and not a jot
Own'd they the lovelorn piteous appeal:

More, more he gaz'd: his human senses reel:
Some hungry spell that loveliness absorbs;
There was no recognition in those orbs.
"Lamia!" he cried - and no soft-toned reply.
The many heard, and the loud revelry
Grew hush; the stately music no more breathes;
The myrtle sicken'd in a thousand wreaths.
By faint degrees, voice, lute, and pleasure ceased;
A deadly silence step by step increased,
Until it seem'd a horrid presence there,
And not a man but felt the terror in his hair.
"Lamia!" he shriek'd; and nothing but the shriek
With its sad echo did the silence break.
"Begone, foul dream!" he cried, gazing again
In the bride's face, where now no azure vein
Wander'd on fair-spaced temples; no soft bloom
Misted the cheek; no passion to illume
The deep-recessed vision - all was blight;
Lamia, no longer fair, there sat a deadly white.
"Shut, shut those juggling eyes, thou ruthless man!
Turn them aside, wretch! or the righteous ban
Of all the Gods, whose dreadful images
Here represent their shadowy presences,
May pierce them on the sudden with the thorn
Of painful blindness; leaving thee forlorn,
In trembling dotage to the feeblest fright
Of conscience, for their long offended might,
For all thine impious proud-heart sophistries,
Unlawful magic, and enticing lies.
Corinthians! look upon that gray-beard wretch!
Mark how, possess'd, his lashless eyelids stretch
Around his demon eyes! Corinthians, see!
My sweet bride withers at their potency."
"Fool!" said the sophist, in an under-tone
Gruff with contempt; which a death-nighing moan
From Lycius answer'd, as heart-struck and lost,

He sank supine beside the aching ghost.
"Fool! Fool!" repeated he, while his eyes still
Relented not, nor mov'd; "from every ill
Of life have I preserv'd thee to this day,
And shall I see thee made a serpent's prey?"
Then Lamia breath'd death breath; the sophist's eye,
Like a sharp spear, went through her utterly,
Keen, cruel, perceant, stinging: she, as well
As her weak hand could any meaning tell,
Motion'd him to be silent; vainly so,
He look'd and look'd again a level - No!
"A Serpent!" echoed he; no sooner said,
Than with a frightful scream she vanished:
And Lycius' arms were empty of delight,
As were his limbs of life, from that same night.
On the high couch he lay! - his friends came round
Supported him - no pulse, or breath they found,
And, in its marriage robe, the heavy body wound.

Bio: John Keats was an English Romantic poet. He was one of the main figures of the second generation of Romantic poets, along with Lord Byron and Percy Bysshe Shelley, despite his work having been in publication for only four years before his death.

QUEEN MAB
Percy Bysshe Shelley

Whose is the love that, gleaming through the world,
Wards off the poisonous arrow of its scorn?
Whose is the warm and partial praise,
Virtue's most sweet reward?

Beneath whose looks did my reviving soul
Riper in truth and virtuous daring grow?
Whose eyes have I gazed fondly on,
And loved mankind the more?

Harriet! on thine: – thou wert my purer mind;
Thou wert the inspiration of my song;
Thine are these early wilding flowers,
Though garlanded by me.

Then press into thy breast this pledge of love;
And know, though time may change and years may roll,
Each floweret gathered in my heart
It consecrates to thine.

I.

How wonderful is Death,
Death, and his brother Sleep!
One, pale as yonder waning moon
With lips of lurid blue;
The other, rosy as the morn
When throned on ocean's wave

It blushes o'er the world;
Yet both so passing wonderful!

Hath then the gloomy Power
Whose reign is in the tainted sepulchres
Seized on her sinless soul?
Must then that peerless form
Which love and admiration cannot view
Without a beating heart, those azure veins
Which steal like streams along a field of snow,
That lovely outline which is fair
As breathing marble, perish?
Must putrefaction's breath
Leave nothing of this heavenly sight
But loathsomeness and ruin?
Spare nothing but a gloomy theme,
On which the lightest heart might moralize?
Or is it only a sweet slumber
Stealing o'er sensation,
Which the breath of roseate morning
Chaseth into darkness?
Will Ianthe wake again,
And give that faithful bosom joy
Whose sleepless spirit waits to catch
Light, life and rapture, from her smile?

Yes! she will wake again,
Although her glowing limbs are motionless,
And silent those sweet lips,
Once breathing eloquence
That might have soothed a tiger's rage
Or thawed the cold heart of a conqueror.
Her dewy eyes are closed,
And on their lids, whose texture fine
Scarce hides the dark blue orbs beneath,
The baby Sleep is pillowed;

Her golden tresses shade
The bosom's stainless pride,
Curling like tendrils of the parasite
Around a marble column.

Hark! whence that rushing sound?
't is like the wondrous strain
That round a lonely ruin swells,
Which, wandering on the echoing shore,
The enthusiast hears at evening;
't is softer than the west wind's sigh;
't is wilder than the unmeasured notes
Of that strange lyre whose strings
The genii of the breezes sweep;
Those lines of rainbow light
Are like the moonbeams when they fall
Through some cathedral window, but the tints
Are such as may not find
Comparison on earth.

Behold the chariot of the Fairy Queen!
Celestial coursers paw the unyielding air;
Their filmy pennons at her word they furl,
And stop obedient to the reins of light;
These the Queen of Spells drew in;
She spread a charm around the spot,
And, leaning graceful from the ethereal car,
Long did she gaze, and silently,
Upon the slumbering maid.

Oh! not the visioned poet in his dreams,
When silvery clouds float through the wildered brain,
When every sight of lovely, wild and grand
Astonishes, enraptures, elevates,
When fancy at a glance combines
The wondrous and the beautiful,-

So bright, so fair, so wild a shape
Hath ever yet beheld,
As that which reined the coursers of the air
And poured the magic of her gaze
Upon the maiden's sleep.

The broad and yellow moon
Shone dimly through her form –
That form of faultless symmetry;
The pearly and pellucid car
Moved not the moonlight's line.
't was not an earthly pageant.
Those, who had looked upon the sight
Passing all human glory,
Saw not the yellow moon,
Saw not the mortal scene,
Heard not the night-wind's rush,
Heard not an earthly sound,
Saw but the fairy pageant,
Heard but the heavenly strains
That filled the lonely dwelling.

The Fairy's frame was slight -yon fibrous cloud,
That catches but the palest tinge of even,
And which the straining eye can hardly seize
When melting into eastern twilight's shadow,
Were scarce so thin, so slight; but the fair star
That gems the glittering coronet of morn,
Sheds not a light so mild, so powerful,
As that which, bursting from the Fairy's form,
Spread a purpureal halo round the scene,
Yet with an undulating motion,
Swayed to her outline gracefully.

From her celestial car
The Fairy Queen descended,

And thrice she waved her wand
Circled with wreaths of amaranth;
Her thin and misty form
Moved with the moving air,
And the clear silver tones,
As thus she spoke, were such
As are unheard by all but gifted ear.

FAIRY

'Stars! your balmiest influence shed!
Elements! your wrath suspend!
Sleep, Ocean, in the rocky bounds
That circle thy domain!
Let not a breath be seen to stir
Around yon grass-grown ruin's height!
Let even the restless gossamer
Sleep on the moveless air!
Soul of Ianthe! thou,
Judged alone worthy of the envied boon
That waits the good and the sincere; that waits
Those who have struggled, and with resolute will
Vanquished earth's pride and meanness, burst the chains,
The icy chains of custom, and have shone
The day-stars of their age; -Soul of
Ianthe!
Awake! arise!'

Sudden arose
Ianthe's Soul; it stood
All beautiful in naked purity,
The perfect semblance of its bodily frame;
Instinct with inexpressible beauty and grace -
Each stain of earthliness
Had passed away -it reassumed
Its native dignity and stood

Immortal amid ruin.

Upon the couch the body lay,
Wrapt in the depth of slumber;
Its features were fixed and meaningless,
Yet animal life was there,
And every organ yet performed
Its natural functions; 'twas a sight
Of wonder to behold the body and the soul.
The self-same lineaments, the same
Marks of identity were there;
Yet, oh, how different! One aspires to Heaven,
Pants for its sempiternal heritage,
And, ever changing, ever rising still,
Wantons in endless being:
The other, for a time the unwilling sport
Of circumstance and passion, struggles on;
Fleets through its sad duration rapidly;
Then like an useless and worn-out machine,
Rots, perishes, and passes.

FAIRY

'Spirit! who hast dived so deep;
Spirit! who hast soared so high;
Thou the fearless, thou the mild,
Accept the boon thy worth hath earned,
Ascend the car with me!'

SPIRIT

'Do I dream? Is this new feeling
But a visioned ghost of slumber?
If indeed I am a soul,
A free, a disembodied soul,
Speak again to me.'

FAIRY

'I am the Fairy Mab: to me 'tis given
The wonders of the human world to keep;
The secrets of the immeasurable past,
In the unfailing consciences of men,
Those stern, unflattering chroniclers, I find;
The future, from the causes which arise
In each event, I gather; not the sting
Which retributive memory implants
In the hard bosom of the selfish man,
Nor that ecstatic and exulting throb
Which virtue's votary feels when he sums up
The thoughts and actions of a well-spent day,
Are unforeseen, unregistered by me;
And it is yet permitted me to rend
The veil of mortal frailty, that the spirit,
Clothed in its changeless purity, may know
How soonest to accomplish the great end
For which it hath its being, and may taste
That peace which in the end all life will share.
This is the meed of virtue; happy Soul,
Ascend the car with me!'

The chains of earth's immurement
Fell from Ianthe's spirit;
They shrank and brake like bandages of straw
Beneath a wakened giant's strength.
She knew her glorious change,
And felt in apprehension uncontrolled
New raptures opening round;
Each day-dream of her mortal life,
Each frenzied vision of the slumbers
That closed each well-spent day,
Seemed now to meet reality.

The Fairy and the Soul proceeded;
The silver clouds disparted;
And as the car of magic they ascended,
Again the speechless music swelled,
Again the coursers of the air
Unfurled their azure pennons, and the Queen,
Shaking the beamy reins,
Bade them pursue their way.

The magic car moved on.
The night was fair, and countless stars
Studded heaven's dark blue vault;
Just o'er the eastern wave
Peeped the first faint smile of morn.
The magic car moved on -
From the celestial hoofs
The atmosphere in flaming sparkles flew,
And where the burning wheels
Eddied above the mountain's loftiest peak,
Was traced a line of lightning.
Now it flew far above a rock,
The utmost verge of earth,
The rival of the Andes, whose dark brow
Lowered o'er the silver sea.

Far, far below the chariot's path,
Calm as a slumbering babe,
Tremendous Ocean lay.
The mirror of its stillness showed
The pale and waning stars,
The chariot's fiery track,
And the gray light of morn
Tinging those fleecy clouds
That canopied the dawn.

Seemed it that the chariot's way

Lay through the midst of an immense concave
Radiant with million constellations, tinged
With shades of infinite color,
And semicircled with a belt
Flashing incessant meteors.

The magic car moved on.
As they approached their goal,
The coursers seemed to gather speed;
The sea no longer was distinguished; earth
Appeared a vast and shadowy sphere;
The sun's unclouded orb
Rolled through the black concave;
Its rays of rapid light
Parted around the chariot's swifter course,
And fell, like ocean's feathery spray
Dashed from the boiling surge
Before a vessel's prow.

The magic car moved on.
Earth's distant orb appeared
The smallest light that twinkles in the heaven;
Whilst round the chariot's way
Innumerable systems rolled
And countless spheres diffused
An ever-varying glory.
It was a sight of wonder: some
Were hornèd like the crescent moon;
Some shed a mild and silver beam
Like Hesperus o'er the western sea;
Some dashed athwart with trains of flame,
Like worlds to death and ruin driven;
Some shone like suns, and as the chariot passed,
Eclipsed all other light.

Spirit of Nature! here -

In this interminable wilderness
Of worlds, at whose immensity
Even soaring fancy staggers,
Here is thy fitting temple!
Yet not the lightest leaf
That quivers to the passing breeze
Is less instinct with thee;
Yet not the meanest worm
That lurks in graves and fattens on the dead,
Less shares thy eternal breath!
Spirit of Nature! thou,
Imperishable as this scene -
Here is thy fitting temple!

II.

If solitude hath ever led thy steps
To the wild ocean's echoing shore,
And thou hast lingered there,
Until the sun's broad orb
Seemed resting on the burnished wave,
Thou must have marked the lines
Of purple gold that motionless
Hung o'er the sinking sphere;
Thou must have marked the billowy clouds,
Edged with intolerable radiancy,
Towering like rocks of jet
Crowned with a diamond wreath;
And yet there is a moment,
When the sun's highest point
Peeps like a star o'er ocean's western edge,
When those far clouds of feathery gold,
Shaded with deepest purple, gleam
Like islands on a dark blue sea;
Then has thy fancy soared above the earth
And furled its wearied wing

Within the Fairy's fane.

Yet not the golden islands
Gleaming in yon flood of light,
Nor the feathery curtains
Stretching o'er the sun's bright couch,
Nor the burnished ocean-waves
Paving that gorgeous dome,
So fair, so wonderful a sight
As Mab's ethereal palace could afford.
Yet likest evening's vault, that faëry Hall!
As Heaven, low resting on the wave, it spread
Its floors of flashing light,
Its vast and azure dome,
Its fertile golden islands
Floating on a silver sea;
Whilst suns their mingling beamings darted
Through clouds of circumambient darkness,
And pearly battlements around
Looked o'er the immense of Heaven.

The magic car no longer moved.
The Fairy and the Spirit
Entered the Hall of Spells.
Those golden clouds
That rolled in glittering billows
Beneath the azure canopy,
With the ethereal footsteps trembled not;
The light and crimson mists,
Floating to strains of thrilling melody
Through that unearthly dwelling,
Yielded to every movement of the will;
Upon their passive swell the Spirit leaned,
And, for the varied bliss that pressed around,
Used not the glorious privilege
Of virtue and of wisdom.

'Spirit!' the Fairy said,
And pointed to the gorgeous dome,
'this is a wondrous sight
And mocks all human grandeur;
But, were it virtue's only meed to dwell
In a celestial palace, all resigned
To pleasurable impulses, immured
Within the prison of itself, the will
Of changeless Nature would be unfulfilled.
Learn to make others happy. Spirit, come!
This is thine high reward: -the past shall rise;
Thou shalt behold the present; I will teach
The secrets of the future.'

The Fairy and the Spirit
Approached the overhanging battlement.
Below lay stretched the universe!
There, far as the remotest line
That bounds imagination's flight,
Countless and unending orbs
In mazy motion intermingled,
Yet still fulfilled immutably
Eternal Nature's law.
Above, below, around,
The circling systems formed
A wilderness of harmony;
Each with undeviating aim,
In eloquent silence, through the depths of space
Pursued its wondrous way.

There was a little light
That twinkled in the misty distance.
None but a spirit's eye
Might ken that rolling orb.
None but a spirit's eye,

And in no other place
But that celestial dwelling, might behold
Each action of this earth's inhabitants.
But matter, space, and time,
In those aërial mansions cease to act;
And all-prevailing wisdom, when it reaps
The harvest of its excellence, o'erbounds
Those obstacles of which an earthly soul
Fears to attempt the conquest.

The Fairy pointed to the earth.
The Spirit's intellectual eye
Its kindred beings recognized.
The thronging thousands, to a passing view,
Seemed like an ant-hill's citizens.
How wonderful! that even
The passions, prejudices, interests,
That sway the meanest being -the weak touch
That moves the finest nerve
And in one human brain
Causes the faintest thought, becomes a link
In the great chain of Nature!

'Behold,' the Fairy cried,
'Palmyra's ruined palaces!
Behold where grandeur frowned!
Behold where pleasure smiled!
What now remains? -the memory
Of senselessness and shame.
What is immortal there?
Nothing -it stands to tell
A melancholy tale, to give
An awful warning; soon
Oblivion will steal silently
The remnant of its fame.
Monarchs and conquerors there

Proud o'er prostrate millions trod -
The earthquakes of the human race;
Like them, forgotten when the ruin
That marks their shock is past.

'Beside the eternal Nile
The Pyramids have risen.
Nile shall pursue his changeless way;
Those Pyramids shall fall.
Yea! not a stone shall stand to tell
The spot whereon they stood;
Their very site shall be forgotten,
As is their builder's name!

'Behold yon sterile spot,
Where now the wandering Arab's tent
Flaps in the desert blast!
There once old Salem's haughty fane
Reared high to heaven its thousand golden domes,
And in the blushing face of day
Exposed its shameful glory.
Oh! many a widow, many an orphan cursed
The building of that fane; and many a father,
Worn out with toil and slavery, implored
The poor man's God to sweep it from the earth
And spare his children the detested task
Of piling stone on stone and poisoning
The choicest days of life
To soothe a dotard's vanity.
There an inhuman and uncultured race
Howled hideous praises to their Demon-God;
They rushed to war, tore from the mother's womb
The unborn child -old age and infancy
Promiscuous perished; their victorious arms
Left not a soul to breathe. Oh! they were fiends!
But what was he who taught them that the God

Of Nature and benevolence had given
A special sanction to the trade of blood?
His name and theirs are fading, and the tales
Of this barbarian nation, which imposture
Recites till terror credits, are pursuing
Itself into forgetfulness.

'Where Athens, Rome, and Sparta stood,
There is a moral desert now.
The mean and miserable huts,
The yet more wretched palaces,
Contrasted with those ancient fanes
Now crumbling to oblivion, -
The long and lonely colonnades
Through which the ghost of Freedom stalks, -
Seem like a well-known tune,
Which in some dear scene we have loved to hear,
Remembered now in sadness.
But, oh! how much more changed,
How gloomier is the contrast
Of human nature there!
Where Socrates expired, a tyrant's slave,
A coward and a fool, spreads death around -
Then, shuddering, meets his own.
Where Cicero and Antoninus lived,
A cowled and hypocritical monk
Prays, curses and deceives.

'Spirit! ten thousand years
Have scarcely passed away,
Since in the waste, where now the savage drinks
His enemy's blood, and, aping Europe's sons,
Wakes the unholy song of war,
Arose a stately city,
Metropolis of the western continent.
There, now, the mossy column-stone,

Indented by time's unrelaxing grasp,
Which once appeared to brave
All, save its country's ruin, -
There the wide forest scene,
Rude in the uncultivated loveliness
Of gardens long run wild, -
Seems, to the unwilling sojourner whose steps
Chance in that desert has delayed,
Thus to have stood since earth was what it is.
Yet once it was the busiest haunt,
Whither, as to a common centre, flocked
Strangers, and ships, and merchandise;
Once peace and freedom blest
The cultivated plain;
But wealth, that curse of man,
Blighted the bud of its prosperity;
Virtue and wisdom, truth and liberty,
Fled, to return not, until man shall know
That they alone can give the bliss
Worthy a soul that claims
Its kindred with eternity.

'There 's not one atom of yon earth
But once was living man;
Nor the minutest drop of rain,
That hangeth in its thinnest cloud,
But flowed in human veins;
And from the burning plains
Where Libyan monsters yell,
From the most gloomy glens
Of Greenland's sunless clime,
To where the golden fields
Of fertile England spread
Their harvest to the day,
Thou canst not find one spot
Whereon no city stood.

'How strange is human pride!
I tell thee that those living things,
To whom the fragile blade of grass
That springeth in the morn
And perisheth ere noon,
Is an unbounded world;
I tell thee that those viewless beings,
Whose mansion is the smallest particle
Of the impassive atmosphere,
Think, feel and live like man;
That their affections and antipathies,
Like his, produce the laws
Ruling their moral state;
And the minutest throb
That through their frame diffuses
The slightest, faintest motion,
Is fixed and indispensable
As the majestic laws
That rule yon rolling orbs.'

The Fairy paused. The Spirit,
In ecstasy of admiration, felt
All knowledge of the past revived; the events
Of old and wondrous times,
Which dim tradition interruptedly
Teaches the credulous vulgar, were unfolded
In just perspective to the view;
Yet dim from their infinitude.
The Spirit seemed to stand
High on an isolated pinnacle;
The flood of ages combating below,
The depth of the unbounded universe
Above, and all around
Nature's unchanging harmony.

III.

'Fairy!' the Spirit said,
And on the Queen of Spells
Fixed her ethereal eyes,
'I thank thee. Thou hast given
A boon which I will not resign, and taught
A lesson not to be unlearned. I know
The past, and thence I will essay to glean
A warning for the future, so that man
May profit by his errors and derive
Experience from his folly;
For, when the power of imparting joy
Is equal to the will, the human soul
Requires no other heaven.'

MAB

'Turn thee, surpassing Spirit!
Much yet remains unscanned.
Thou knowest how great is man,
Thou knowest his imbecility;
Yet learn thou what he is;
Yet learn the lofty destiny
Which restless Time prepares
For every living soul.

'Behold a gorgeous palace that amid
Yon populous city rears its thousand towers
And seems itself a city. Gloomy troops
Of sentinels in stern and silent ranks
Encompass it around; the dweller there
Cannot be free and happy; hearest thou not
The curses of the fatherless, the groans
Of those who have no friend? He passes on -
The King, the wearer of a gilded chain

That binds his soul to abjectness, the fool
Whom courtiers nickname monarch, whilst a slave
Even to the basest appetites -that man
Heeds not the shriek of penury; he smiles
At the deep curses which the destitute
Mutter in secret, and a sullen joy
Pervades his bloodless heart when thousands groan
But for those morsels which his wantonness
Wastes in unjoyous revelry, to save
All that they love from famine; when he hears
The tale of horror, to some ready-made face
Of hypocritical assent he turns,
Smothering the glow of shame, that, spite of him,
Flushes his bloated cheek.

Now to the meal
Of silence, grandeur and excess he drags
His palled unwilling appetite. If gold,
Gleaming around, and numerous viands culled
From every clime could force the loathing sense
To overcome satiety, -if wealth
The spring it draws from poisons not, -or vice,
Unfeeling, stubborn vice, converteth not
Its food to deadliest venom; then that king
Is happy; and the peasant who fulfils
His unforced task, when he returns at even
And by the blazing fagot meets again
Her welcome for whom all his toil is sped,
Tastes not a sweeter meal.

Behold him now
Stretched on the gorgeous couch; his fevered brain
Reels dizzily awhile; but ah! too soon
The slumber of intemperance subsides,
And conscience, that undying serpent, calls
Her venomous brood to their nocturnal task.

Listen! he speaks! oh! mark that frenzied eye -
Oh! mark that deadly visage!'

KING

'No cessation!
Oh! must this last forever! Awful death,
I wish, yet fear to clasp thee! -Not one moment
Of dreamless sleep! O dear and blessèd Peace,
Why dost thou shroud thy vestal purity
In penury and dungeons? Wherefore lurkest
With danger, death, and solitude; yet shun'st
The palace I have built thee? Sacred Peace!
Oh, visit me but once, -but pitying shed
One drop of balm upon my withered soul!'

THE FAIRY

'Vain man! that palace is the virtuous heart,
And Peace defileth not her snowy robes
In such a shed as thine. Hark! yet he mutters;
His slumbers are but varied agonies;
They prey like scorpions on the springs of life.
There needeth not the hell that bigots frame
To punish those who err; earth in itself
Contains at once the evil and the cure;
And all-sufficing Nature can chastise
Those who transgress her law; she only knows
How justly to proportion to the fault
The punishment it merits.

Is it strange
That this poor wretch should pride him in his woe?
Take pleasure in his abjectness, and hug
The scorpion that consumes him? Is it strange
That, placed on a conspicuous throne of thorns,

Grasping an iron sceptre, and immured
Within a splendid prison whose stern bounds
Shut him from all that's good or dear on earth,
His soul asserts not its humanity?
That man's mild nature rises not in war
Against a king's employ? No -'tis not strange.
He, like the vulgar, thinks, feels, acts, and lives
Just as his father did; the unconquered powers
Of precedent and custom interpose
Between a king and virtue. Stranger yet,
To those who know not Nature nor deduce
The future from the present, it may seem,
That not one slave, who suffers from the crimes
Of this unnatural being, not one wretch,
Whose children famish and whose nuptial bed
Is earth's unpitying bosom, rears an arm
To dash him from his throne!

Those gilded flies
That, basking in the sunshine of a court,
Fatten on its corruption! what are they? -
The drones of the community; they feed
On the mechanic's labor; the starved hind
For them compels the stubborn glebe to yield
Its unshared harvests; and yon squalid form,
Leaner than fleshless misery, that wastes
A sunless life in the unwholesome mine,
Drags out in labor a protracted death
To glut their grandeur; many faint with toil
That few may know the cares and woe of sloth.

Whence, thinkest thou, kings and parasites arose?
Whence that unnatural line of drones who heap
Toil and unvanquishable penury
On those who build their palaces and bring
Their daily bread? -From vice, black loathsome vice;

From rapine, madness, treachery, and wrong;
From all that genders misery, and makes
Of earth this thorny wilderness; from lust,
Revenge, and murder. -And when reason's voice,
Loud as the voice of Nature, shall have waked
The nations; and mankind perceive that vice
Is discord, war and misery; that virtue
Is peace and happiness and harmony;
When man's maturer nature shall disdain
The playthings of its childhood; -kingly glare
Will lose its power to dazzle, its authority
Will silently pass by; the gorgeous throne
Shall stand unnoticed in the regal hall,
Fast falling to decay; whilst falsehood's trade
Shall be as hateful and unprofitable
As that of truth is now.

Where is the fame
Which the vain-glorious mighty of the earth
Seek to eternize? Oh! the faintest sound
From time's light footfall, the minutest wave
That swells the flood of ages, whelms in nothing
The unsubstantial bubble. Ay! to-day
Stern is the tyrant's mandate, red the gaze
That flashes desolation, strong the arm
That scatters multitudes. To-morrow comes!
That mandate is a thunder-peal that died
In ages past; that gaze, a transient flash
On which the midnight closed; and on that arm
The worm has made his meal.

The virtuous man,
Who, great in his humility as kings
Are little in their grandeur; he who leads
Invincibly a life of resolute good
And stands amid the silent dungeon-depths

More free and fearless than the trembling judge
Who, clothed in venal power, vainly strove
To bind the impassive spirit; -when he falls,
His mild eye beams benevolence no more;
Withered the hand outstretched but to relieve;
Sunk reason's simple eloquence that rolled
But to appall the guilty. Yes! the grave
Hath quenched that eye and death's relentless frost
Withered that arm; but the unfading fame
Which virtue hangs upon its votary's tomb,
The deathless memory of that man whom kings
Call to their minds and tremble, the remembrance
With which the happy spirit contemplates
Its well-spent pilgrimage on earth,
Shall never pass away.

'Nature rejects the monarch, not the man;
The subject, not the citizen; for kings
And subjects, mutual foes, forever play
A losing game into each other's hands,
Whose stakes are vice and misery. The man
Of virtuous soul commands not, nor obeys.
Power, like a desolating pestilence,
Pollutes whate'er it touches; and obedience,
Bane of all genius, virtue, freedom, truth,
Makes slaves of men, and of the human frame
A mechanized automaton.

When Nero
High over flaming Rome with savage joy
Lowered like a fiend, drank with enraptured ear
The shrieks of agonizing death, beheld
The frightful desolation spread, and felt
A new-created sense within his soul
Thrill to the sight and vibrate to the sound, -
Thinkest thou his grandeur had not overcome

The force of human kindness? And when Rome
With one stern blow hurled not the tyrant down,
Crushed not the arm red with her dearest blood,
Had not submissive abjectness destroyed
Nature's suggestions?

Look on yonder earth:
The golden harvests spring; the unfailing sun
Sheds light and life; the fruits, the flowers, the trees,
Arise in due succession; all things speak
Peace, harmony and love. The universe,
In Nature's silent eloquence, declares
That all fulfil the works of love and joy, -
All but the outcast, Man. He fabricates
The sword which stabs his peace; he cherisheth
The snakes that gnaw his heart; he raiseth up
The tyrant whose delight is in his woe,
Whose sport is in his agony. Yon sun,
Lights it the great alone? Yon silver beams,
Sleep they less sweetly on the cottage thatch
Than on the dome of kings? Is mother earth
A step-dame to her numerous sons who earn
Her unshared gifts with unremitting toil;
A mother only to those puling babes
Who, nursed in ease and luxury, make men
The playthings of their babyhood and mar
In self-important childishness that peace
Which men alone appreciate?

'Spirit of Nature, no!
The pure diffusion of thy essence throbs
Alike in every human heart.
Thou aye erectest there
Thy throne of power unappealable;
Thou art the judge beneath whose nod
Man's brief and frail authority

Is powerless as the wind
That passeth idly by;
Thine the tribunal which surpasseth
The show of human justice
As God surpasses man!

'Spirit of Nature! thou
Life of interminable multitudes;
Soul of those mighty spheres
Whose changeless paths through Heaven's deep silence lie;
Soul of that smallest being,
The dwelling of whose life
Is one faint April sun-gleam; -
Man, like these passive things,
Thy will unconsciously fulfilleth;
Like theirs, his age of endless peace,
Which time is fast maturing,
Will swiftly, surely, come;
And the unbounded frame which thou pervadest,
Will be without a flaw
Marring its perfect symmetry!

IV.

'How beautiful this night! the balmiest sigh,
Which vernal zephyrs breathe in evening's ear,
Were discord to the speaking quietude
That wraps this moveless scene. Heaven's ebon vault,
Studded with stars unutterably bright,
Through which the moon's unclouded grandeur rolls,
Seems like a canopy which love had spread
To curtain her sleeping world. Yon gentle hills,
Robed in a garment of untrodden snow;
Yon darksome rocks, whence icicles depend
So stainless that their white and glittering spires
Tinge not the moon's pure beam; yon castled steep

Whose banner hangeth o'er the time-worn tower
So idly that rapt fancy deemeth it
A metaphor of peace; -all form a scene
Where musing solitude might love to lift
Her soul above this sphere of earthliness;
Where silence undisturbed might watch alone -
So cold, so bright, so still.

The orb of day
In southern climes o'er ocean's waveless field
Sinks sweetly smiling; not the faintest breath
Steals o'er the unruffled deep; the clouds of eve
Reflect unmoved the lingering beam of day;
And Vesper's image on the western main
Is beautifully still. To-morrow comes:
Cloud upon cloud, in dark and deepening mass,
Roll o'er the blackened waters; the deep roar
Of distant thunder mutters awfully;
Tempest unfolds its pinion o'er the gloom
That shrouds the boiling surge; the pitiless fiend,
With all his winds and lightnings, tracks his prey;
The torn deep yawns, -the vessel finds a grave
Beneath its jagged gulf.

Ah! whence yon glare
That fires the arch of heaven? that dark red smoke
Blotting the silver moon? The stars are quenched
In darkness, and the pure and spangling snow
Gleams faintly through the gloom that gathers round.
Hark to that roar whose swift and deafening peals
In countless echoes through the mountains ring,
Startling pale Midnight on her starry throne!
Now swells the intermingling din; the jar
Frequent and frightful of the bursting bomb;
The falling beam, the shriek, the groan, the shout,
The ceaseless clangor, and the rush of men

Inebriate with rage: -loud and more loud
The discord grows; till pale Death shuts the scene
And o'er the conqueror and the conquered draws
His cold and bloody shroud. -Of all the men
Whom day's departing beam saw blooming there
In proud and vigorous health; of all the hearts
That beat with anxious life at sunset there;
How few survive, how few are beating now!
All is deep silence, like the fearful calm
That slumbers in the storm's portentous pause;
Save when the frantic wail of widowed love
Comes shuddering on the blast, or the faint moan
With which some soul bursts from the frame of clay
Wrapt round its struggling powers.

The gray morn
Dawns on the mournful scene; the sulphurous smoke
Before the icy wind slow rolls away,
And the bright beams of frosty morning dance
Along the spangling snow. There tracks of blood
Even to the forest's depth, and scattered arms,
And lifeless warriors, whose hard lineaments
Death's self could change not, mark the dreadful path
Of the outsallying victors; far behind
Black ashes note where their proud city stood.
Within yon forest is a gloomy glen -
Each tree which guards its darkness from the day,
Waves o'er a warrior's tomb.

I see thee shrink,
Surpassing Spirit! -wert thou human else?
I see a shade of doubt and horror fleet
Across thy stainless features; yet fear not;
This is no unconnected misery,
Nor stands uncaused and irretrievable.
Man's evil nature, that apology

Which kings who rule, and cowards who crouch, set up
For their unnumbered crimes, sheds not the blood
Which desolates the discord-wasted land.
From kings and priests and statesmen war arose,
Whose safety is man's deep unbettered woe,
Whose grandeur his debasement. Let the axe
Strike at the root, the poison-tree will fall;
And where its venomed exhalations spread
Ruin, and death, and woe, where millions lay
Quenching the serpent's famine, and their bones
Bleaching unburied in the putrid blast,
A garden shall arise, in loveliness
Surpassing fabled Eden.

Hath Nature's soul, -
That formed this world so beautiful, that spread
Earth's lap with plenty, and life's smallest chord
Strung to unchanging unison, that gave
The happy birds their dwelling in the grove,
That yielded to the wanderers of the deep
The lovely silence of the unfathomed main,
And filled the meanest worm that crawls in dust
With spirit, thought and love, -on Man alone,
Partial in causeless malice, wantonly
Heaped ruin, vice, and slavery; his soul
Blasted with withering curses; placed afar
The meteor-happiness, that shuns his grasp,
But serving on the frightful gulf to glare
Rent wide beneath his footsteps?

Nature! -no!
Kings, priests and statesmen blast the human flower
Even in its tender bud; their influence darts
Like subtle poison through the bloodless veins
Of desolate society. The child,
Ere he can lisp his mother's sacred name,

Swells with the unnatural pride of crime, and lifts
His baby-sword even in a hero's mood.
This infant arm becomes the bloodiest scourge
Of devastated earth; whilst specious names,
Learnt in soft childhood's unsuspecting hour,
Serve as the sophisms with which manhood dims
Bright reason's ray and sanctifies the sword
Upraised to shed a brother's innocent blood.
Let priest-led slaves cease to proclaim that man
Inherits vice and misery, when force
And falsehood hang even o'er the cradled babe,
Stifling with rudest grasp all natural good.

'Ah! to the stranger-soul, when first it peeps
From its new tenement and looks abroad
For happiness and sympathy, how stern
And desolate a tract is this wide world!
How withered all the buds of natural good!
No shade, no shelter from the sweeping storms
Of pitiless power! On its wretched frame
Poisoned, perchance, by the disease and woe
Heaped on the wretched parent whence it sprung
By morals, law and custom, the pure winds
Of heaven, that renovate the insect tribes,
May breathe not. The untainting light of day
May visit not its longings. It is bound
Ere it has life; yea, all the chains are forged
Long ere its being; all liberty and love
And peace is torn from its defencelessness;
Cursed from its birth, even from its cradle doomed
To abjectness and bondage!

'Throughout this varied and eternal world
Soul is the only element, the block
That for uncounted ages has remained.
The moveless pillar of a mountain's weight

Is active living spirit. Every grain
Is sentient both in unity and part,
And the minutest atom comprehends
A world of loves and hatreds; these beget
Evil and good; hence truth and falsehood spring;
Hence will and thought and action, all the germs
Of pain or pleasure, sympathy or hate,
That variegate the eternal universe.
Soul is not more polluted than the beams
Of heaven's pure orb ere round their rapid lines
The taint of earth-born atmospheres arise.

'Man is of soul and body, formed for deeds
Of high resolve; on fancy's boldest wing
To soar unwearied, fearlessly to turn
The keenest pangs to peacefulness, and taste
The joys which mingled sense and spirit yield;
Or he is formed for abjectness and woe,
To grovel on the dunghill of his fears,
To shrink at every sound, to quench the flame
Of natural love in sensualism, to know
That hour as blest when on his worthless days
The frozen hand of death shall set its seal,
Yet fear the cure, though hating the disease.
The one is man that shall hereafter be;
The other, man as vice has made him now.

'War is the statesman's game, the priest's delight,
The lawyer's jest, the hired assassin's trade,
And to those royal murderers whose mean thrones
Are bought by crimes of treachery and gore,
The bread they eat, the staff on which they lean.
Guards, garbed in blood-red livery, surround
Their palaces, participate the crimes
That force defends and from a nation's rage
Secures the crown, which all the curses reach

That famine, frenzy, woe and penury breathe.
These are the hired bravos who defend
The tyrant's throne -the bullies of his fear;
These are the sinks and channels of worst vice,
The refuse of society, the dregs
Of all that is most vile; their cold hearts blend
Deceit with sternness, ignorance with pride,
All that is mean and villainous with rage
Which hopelessness of good and self-contempt
Alone might kindle; they are decked in wealth,
Honor and power, then are sent abroad
To do their work. The pestilence that stalks
In gloomy triumph through some eastern land
Is less destroying. They cajole with gold
And promises of fame the thoughtless youth
Already crushed with servitude; he knows
His wretchedness too late, and cherishes
Repentance for his ruin, when his doom
Is sealed in gold and blood!
Those too the tyrant serve, who, skilled to snare
The feet of justice in the toils of law,
Stand ready to oppress the weaker still,
And right or wrong will vindicate for gold,
Sneering at public virtue, which beneath
Their pitiless tread lies torn and trampled where
Honor sits smiling at the sale of truth.

'Then grave and hoary-headed hypocrites,
Without a hope, a passion or a love,
Who through a life of luxury and lies
Have crept by flattery to the seats of power,
Support the system whence their honors flow.
They have three words -well tyrants know their use,
Well pay them for the loan with usury
Torn from a bleeding world! -God, Hell and Heaven:
A vengeful, pitiless, and almighty fiend,

Whose mercy is a nickname for the rage
Of tameless tigers hungering for blood;
Hell, a red gulf of everlasting fire,
Where poisonous and undying worms prolong
Eternal misery to those hapless slaves
Whose life has been a penance for its crimes;
And Heaven, a meed for those who dare belie
Their human nature, quake, believe and cringe
Before the mockeries of earthly power.

'These tools the tyrant tempers to his work,
Wields in his wrath, and as he wills destroys,
Omnipotent in wickedness; the while
Youth springs, age moulders, manhood tamely does
His bidding, bribed by short-lived joys to lend
Force to the weakness of his trembling arm.
They rise, they fall; one generation comes
Yielding its harvest to destruction's scythe.
It fades, another blossoms; yet behold!
Red glows the tyrant's stamp-mark on its bloom,
Withering and cankering deep its passive prime.
He has invented lying words and modes,
Empty and vain as his own coreless heart;
Evasive meanings, nothings of much sound,
To lure the heedless victim to the toils
Spread round the valley of its paradise.

'Look to thyself, priest, conqueror or prince!
Whether thy trade is falsehood, and thy lusts
Deep wallow in the earnings of the poor,
With whom thy master was; or thou delight'st
In numbering o'er the myriads of thy slain,
All misery weighing nothing in the scale
Against thy short-lived fame; or thou dost load
With cowardice and crime the groaning land,
A pomp-fed king. Look to thy wretched self!

Ay, art thou not the veriest slave that e'er
Crawled on the loathing earth? Are not thy days
Days of unsatisfying listlessness?
Dost thou not cry, ere night's long rack is o'er,
"When will the morning come?" Is not thy youth
A vain and feverish dream of sensualism?
Thy manhood blighted with unripe disease?
Are not thy views of unregretted death
Drear, comfortless and horrible? Thy mind,
Is it not morbid as thy nerveless frame,
Incapable of judgment, hope or love?
And dost thou wish the errors to survive,
That bar thee from all sympathies of good,
After the miserable interest
Thou hold'st in their protraction? When the grave
Has swallowed up thy memory and thyself,
Dost thou desire the bane that poisons earth
To twine its roots around thy coffined clay,
Spring from thy bones, and blossom on thy tomb,
That of its fruit thy babes may eat and die?

V.

'Thus do the generations of the earth
Go to the grave and issue from the womb,
Surviving still the imperishable change
That renovates the world; even as the leaves
Which the keen frost-wind of the waning year
Has scattered on the forest-soil and heaped
For many seasons there -though long they choke,
Loading with loathsome rottenness the land,
All germs of promise, yet when the tall trees
From which they fell, shorn of their lovely shapes,
Lie level with the earth to moulder there,
They fertilize the land they long deformed;
Till from the breathing lawn a forest springs

Of youth, integrity and loveliness,
Like that which gave it life, to spring and die.
Thus suicidal selfishness, that blights
The fairest feelings of the opening heart,
Is destined to decay, whilst from the soil
Shall spring all virtue, all delight, all love,
And judgment cease to wage unnatural war
With passion's unsubduable array.
Twin-sister of Religion, Selfishness!
Rival in crime and falsehood, aping all
The wanton horrors of her bloody play;
Yet frozen, unimpassioned, spiritless,
Shunning the light, and owning not its name,
Compelled by its deformity to screen
With flimsy veil of justice and of right
Its unattractive lineaments that scare
All save the brood of ignorance; at once
The cause and the effect of tyranny;
Unblushing, hardened, sensual and vile;
Dead to all love but of its abjectness;
With heart impassive by more noble powers
Than unshared pleasure, sordid gain, or fame;
Despising its own miserable being,
Which still it longs, yet fears, to disenthrall.

'Hence commerce springs, the venal interchange
Of all that human art or Nature yield;
Which wealth should purchase not, but want demand,
And natural kindness hasten to supply
From the full fountain of its boundless love,
Forever stifled, drained and tainted now.
Commerce! beneath whose poison-breathing shade
No solitary virtue dares to spring,
But poverty and wealth with equal hand
Scatter their withering curses, and unfold
The doors of premature and violent death

To pining famine and full-fed disease,
To all that shares the lot of human life,
Which, poisoned body and soul, scarce drags the chain
That lengthens as it goes and clanks behind.

'Commerce has set the mark of selfishness,
The signet of its all-enslaving power,
Upon a shining ore, and called it gold;
Before whose image bow the vulgar great,
The vainly rich, the miserable proud,
The mob of peasants, nobles, priests and kings,
And with blind feelings reverence the power
That grinds them to the dust of misery.
But in the temple of their hireling hearts
Gold is a living god and rules in scorn
All earthly things but virtue.

'Since tyrants by the sale of human life
Heap luxuries to their sensualism, and fame
To their wide-wasting and insatiate pride,
Success has sanctioned to a credulous world
The ruin, the disgrace, the woe of war.
His hosts of blind and unresisting dupes
The despot numbers; from his cabinet
These puppets of his schemes he moves at will,
Even as the slaves by force or famine driven,
Beneath a vulgar master, to perform
A task of cold and brutal drudgery; -
Hardened to hope, insensible to fear,
Scarce living pulleys of a dead machine,
Mere wheels of work and articles of trade,
That grace the proud and noisy pomp of wealth!

'The harmony and happiness of man
Yields to the wealth of nations; that which lifts
His nature to the heaven of its pride,

Is bartered for the poison of his soul;
The weight that drags to earth his towering hopes,
Blighting all prospect but of selfish gain,
Withering all passion but of slavish fear,
Extinguishing all free and generous love
Of enterprise and daring, even the pulse
That fancy kindles in the beating heart
To mingle with sensation, it destroys, -
Leaves nothing but the sordid lust of self,
The grovelling hope of interest and gold,
Unqualified, unmingled, unredeemed
Even by hypocrisy.

And statesmen boast
Of wealth! The wordy eloquence that lives
After the ruin of their hearts, can gild
The bitter poison of a nation's woe;
Can turn the worship of the servile mob
To their corrupt and glaring idol, fame,
From virtue, trampled by its iron tread, -
Although its dazzling pedestal be raised
Amid the horrors of a limb-strewn field,
With desolated dwellings smoking round.
The man of ease, who, by his warm fireside,
To deeds of charitable intercourse
And bare fulfilment of the common laws
Of decency and prejudice confines
The struggling nature of his human heart,
Is duped by their cold sophistry; he sheds
A passing tear perchance upon the wreck
Of earthly peace, when near his dwelling's door
The frightful waves are driven, -when his son
Is murdered by the tyrant, or religion
Drives his wife raving mad. But the poor man
Whose life is misery, and fear and care;
Whom the morn wakens but to fruitless toil;

Who ever hears his famished offspring's scream;
Whom their pale mother's uncomplaining gaze
Forever meets, and the proud rich man's eye
Flashing command, and the heart-breaking scene
Of thousands like himself; -he little heeds
The rhetoric of tyranny; his hate
Is quenchless as his wrongs; he laughs to scorn
The vain and bitter mockery of words,
Feeling the horror of the tyrant's deeds,
And unrestrained but by the arm of power,
That knows and dreads his enmity.

'The iron rod of penury still compels
Her wretched slave to bow the knee to wealth,
And poison, with unprofitable toil,
A life too void of solace to confirm
The very chains that bind him to his doom.
Nature, impartial in munificence,
Has gifted man with all-subduing will.
Matter, with all its transitory shapes,
Lies subjected and plastic at his feet,
That, weak from bondage, tremble as they tread.
How many a rustic Milton has passed by,
Stifling the speechless longings of his heart,
In unremitting drudgery and care!
How many a vulgar Cato has compelled
His energies, no longer tameless then,
To mould a pin or fabricate a nail!
How many a Newton, to whose passive ken
Those mighty spheres that gem infinity
Were only specks of tinsel fixed in heaven
To light the midnights of his native town!

'Yet every heart contains perfection's germ.
The wisest of the sages of the earth,
That ever from the stores of reason drew

Science and truth, and virtue's dreadless tone,
Were but a weak and inexperienced boy,
Proud, sensual, unimpassioned, unimbued
With pure desire and universal love,
Compared to that high being, of cloudless brain,
Untainted passion, elevated will,
Which death (who even would linger long in awe
Within his noble presence and beneath
His changeless eye-beam) might alone subdue.
Him, every slave now dragging through the filth
Of some corrupted city his sad life,
Pining with famine, swoln with luxury,
Blunting the keenness of his spiritual sense
With narrow schemings and unworthy cares,
Or madly rushing through all violent crime
To move the deep stagnation of his soul, -
Might imitate and equal.

But mean lust
Has bound its chains so tight about the earth
That all within it but the virtuous man
Is venal; gold or fame will surely reach
The price prefixed by Selfishness to all
But him of resolute and unchanging will;
Whom nor the plaudits of a servile crowd,
Nor the vile joys of tainting luxury,
Can bribe to yield his elevated soul
To Tyranny or Falsehood, though they wield
With blood-red hand the sceptre of the world.

'All things are sold: the very light of heaven
Is venal; earth's unsparing gifts of love,
The smallest and most despicable things
That lurk in the abysses of the deep,
All objects of our life, even life itself,
And the poor pittance which the laws allow

Of liberty, the fellowship of man,
Those duties which his heart of human love
Should urge him to perform instinctively,
Are bought and sold as in a public mart
Of undisguising Selfishness, that sets
On each its price, the stamp-mark of her reign.
Even love is sold; the solace of all woe
Is turned to deadliest agony, old age
Shivers in selfish beauty's loathing arms,
And youth's corrupted impulses prepare
A life of horror from the blighting bane
Of commerce; whilst the pestilence that springs
From unenjoying sensualism, has filled
All human life with hydra-headed woes.

'Falsehood demands but gold to pay the pangs
Of outraged conscience; for the slavish priest
Sets no great value on his hireling faith;
A little passing pomp, some servile souls,
Whom cowardice itself might safely chain
Or the spare mite of avarice could bribe
To deck the triumph of their languid zeal,
Can make him minister to tyranny.
More daring crime requires a loftier meed.
Without a shudder the slave-soldier lends
His arm to murderous deeds, and steels his heart,
When the dread eloquence of dying men,
Low mingling on the lonely field of fame,
Assails that nature whose applause he sells
For the gross blessings of the patriot mob,
For the vile gratitude of heartless kings,
And for a cold world's good word, -viler still!

'There is a nobler glory which survives
Until our being fades, and, solacing
All human care, accompanies its change;

Deserts not virtue in the dungeon's gloom,
And in the precincts of the palace guides
Its footsteps through that labyrinth of crime;
Imbues his lineaments with dauntlessness,
Even when from power's avenging hand he takes
Its sweetest, last and noblest title -death;
-The consciousness of good, which neither gold,
Nor sordid fame, nor hope of heavenly bliss,
Can purchase; but a life of resolute good,
Unalterable will, quenchless desire
Of universal happiness, the heart
That beats with it in unison, the brain
Whose ever-wakeful wisdom toils to change
Reason's rich stores for its eternal weal.

'This commerce of sincerest virtue needs
No meditative signs of selfishness,
No jealous intercourse of wretched gain,
No balancings of prudence, cold and long;
In just and equal measure all is weighed,
One scale contains the sum of human weal,
And one, the good man's heart.

How vainly seek
The selfish for that happiness denied
To aught but virtue! Blind and hardened, they,
Who hope for peace amid the storms of care,
Who covet power they know not how to use,
And sigh for pleasure they refuse to give, -
Madly they frustrate still their own designs;
And, where they hope that quiet to enjoy
Which virtue pictures, bitterness of soul,
Pining regrets, and vain repentances,
Disease, disgust and lassitude pervade
Their valueless and miserable lives.

'But hoary-headed selfishness has felt
Its death-blow and is tottering to the grave;
A brighter morn awaits the human day,
When every transfer of earth's natural gifts
Shall be a commerce of good words and works;
When poverty and wealth, the thirst of fame,
The fear of infamy, disease and woe,
War with its million horrors, and fierce hell,
Shall live but in the memory of time,
Who, like a penitent libertine, shall start,
Look back, and shudder at his younger years.'

VI.

All touch, all eye, all ear,
The Spirit felt the Fairy's burning speech.
O'er the thin texture of its frame
The varying periods painted changing glows,
As on a summer even,
When soul-enfolding music floats around,
The stainless mirror of the lake
Re-images the eastern gloom,
Mingling convulsively its purple hues
With sunset's burnished gold.
Then thus the Spirit spoke:
'It is a wild and miserable world!
Thorny, and full of care,
Which every fiend can make his prey at will!
O Fairy! in the lapse of years,
Is there no hope in store?
Will yon vast suns roll on
Interminably, still illuming
The night of so many wretched souls,
And see no hope for them?
Will not the universal Spirit e'er
Revivify this withered limb of Heaven?'

The Fairy calmly smiled
In comfort, and a kindling gleam of hope
Suffused the Spirit's lineaments.
'Oh! rest thee tranquil; chase those fearful doubts
Which ne'er could rack an everlasting soul
That sees the chains which bind it to its doom.
Yes! crime and misery are in yonder earth,
Falsehood, mistake and lust;
But the eternal world
Contains at once the evil and the cure.
Some eminent in virtue shall start up,
Even in perversest time;
The truths of their pure lips, that never die,
Shall bind the scorpion falsehood with a wreath
Of ever-living flame,
Until the monster sting itself to death.

'How sweet a scene will earth become!
Of purest spirits a pure dwelling-place,
Symphonious with the planetary spheres;
When man, with changeless Nature coalescing,
Will undertake regeneration's work,
When its ungenial poles no longer point
To the red and baleful sun
That faintly twinkles there!

'Spirit, on yonder earth,
Falsehood now triumphs; deadly power
Has fixed its seal upon the lip of truth!
Madness and misery are there!
The happiest is most wretched! Yet confide
Until pure health-drops from the cup of joy
Fall like a dew of balm upon the world.
Now, to the scene I show, in silence turn,
And read the blood-stained charter of all woe,

Which Nature soon with recreating hand
Will blot in mercy from the book of earth.
How bold the flight of passion's wandering wing,
How swift the step of reason's firmer tread,
How calm and sweet the victories of life,
How terrorless the triumph of the grave!
How powerless were the mightiest monarch's arm,
Vain his loud threat, and impotent his frown!
How ludicrous the priest's dogmatic roar!
The weight of his exterminating curse
How light! and his affected charity,
To suit the pressure of the changing times,
What palpable deceit! -but for thy aid,
Religion! but for thee, prolific fiend,
Who peoplest earth with demons, hell with men,
And heaven with slaves!

'Thou taintest all thou lookest upon! -the stars,
Which on thy cradle beamed so brightly sweet,
Were gods to the distempered playfulness
Of thy untutored infancy; the trees,
The grass, the clouds, the mountains and the sea,
All living things that walk, swim, creep or fly,
Were gods; the sun had homage, and the moon
Her worshipper. Then thou becamest, a boy,
More daring in thy frenzies; every shape,
Monstrous or vast, or beautifully wild,
Which from sensation's relics fancy culls;
The spirits of the air, the shuddering ghost,
The genii of the elements, the powers
That give a shape to Nature's varied works,
Had life and place in the corrupt belief
Of thy blind heart; yet still thy youthful hands
Were pure of human blood. Then manhood gave
Its strength and ardor to thy frenzied brain;
Thine eager gaze scanned the stupendous scene,

Whose wonders mocked the knowledge of thy pride;
Their everlasting and unchanging laws
Reproached thine ignorance. Awhile thou stood'st
Baffled and gloomy; then thou didst sum up
The elements of all that thou didst know;
The changing seasons, winter's leafless reign,
The budding of the heaven-breathing trees,
The eternal orbs that beautify the night,
The sunrise, and the setting of the moon,
Earthquakes and wars, and poisons and disease,
And all their causes, to an abstract point
Converging thou didst bend, and called it God!
The self-sufficing, the omnipotent,
The merciful, and the avenging God!
Who, prototype of human misrule, sits
High in heaven's realm, upon a golden throne,
Even like an earthly king; and whose dread work,
Hell, gapes forever for the unhappy slaves
Of fate, whom he created in his sport
To triumph in their torments when they fell!
Earth heard the name; earth trembled as the smoke
Of his revenge ascended up to heaven,
Blotting the constellations; and the cries
Of millions butchered in sweet confidence
And unsuspecting peace, even when the bonds
Of safety were confirmed by wordy oaths
Sworn in his dreadful name, rung through the land;
Whilst innocent babes writhed on thy stubborn spear,
And thou didst laugh to hear the mother's shriek
Of maniac gladness, as the sacred steel
Felt cold in her torn entrails!

'Religion! thou wert then in manhood's prime;
But age crept on; one God would not suffice
For senile puerility; thou framedst
A tale to suit thy dotage and to glut

Thy misery-thirsting soul, that the mad fiend
Thy wickedness had pictured might afford
A plea for sating the unnatural thirst
For murder, rapine, violence and crime,
That still consumed thy being, even when
Thou heard'st the step of fate; that flames might light
Thy funeral scene; and the shrill horrent shrieks
Of parents dying on the pile that burned
To light their children to thy paths, the roar
Of the encircling flames, the exulting cries
Of thine apostles loud commingling there,
Might sate thine hungry ear
Even on the bed of death!

'But now contempt is mocking thy gray hairs;
Thou art descending to the darksome grave,
Unhonored and unpitied but by those
Whose pride is passing by like thine, and sheds,
Like thine, a glare that fades before the sun
Of truth, and shines but in the dreadful night
That long has lowered above the ruined world.

'Throughout these infinite orbs of mingling light
Of which yon earth is one, is wide diffused
A Spirit of activity and life,
That knows no term, cessation or decay;
That fades not when the lamp of earthly life,
Extinguished in the dampness of the grave,
Awhile there slumbers, more than when the babe
In the dim newness of its being feels
The impulses of sublunary things,
And all is wonder to unpractised sense;
But, active, steadfast and eternal, still
Guides the fierce whirlwind, in the tempest roars,
Cheers in the day, breathes in the balmy groves,
Strengthens in health, and poisons in disease;

And in the storm of change, that ceaselessly
Rolls round the eternal universe and shakes
Its undecaying battlement, presides,
Apportioning with irresistible law
The place each spring of its machine shall fill;
So that, when waves on waves tumultuous heap
Confusion to the clouds, and fiercely driven
Heaven's lightnings scorch the uprooted ocean-fords -
Whilst, to the eye of shipwrecked mariner,
Lone sitting on the bare and shuddering rock,
All seems unlinked contingency and chance –
No atom of this turbulence fulfils
A vague and unnecessitated task
Or acts but as it must and ought to act.
Even the minutest molecule of light,
That in an April sunbeam's fleeting glow
Fulfils its destined though invisible work,
The universal Spirit guides; nor less
When merciless ambition, or mad zeal,
Has led two hosts of dupes to battle-field,
That, blind, they there may dig each other's graves
And call the sad work glory, does it rule
All passions; not a thought, a will, an act,
No working of the tyrant's moody mind,
Nor one misgiving of the slaves who boast
Their servitude to hide the shame they feel,
Nor the events enchaining every will,
That from the depths of unrecorded time
Have drawn all-influencing virtue, pass
Unrecognized or unforeseen by thee,
Soul of the Universe! eternal spring
Of life and death, of happiness and woe,
Of all that chequers the phantasmal scene
That floats before our eyes in wavering light,
Which gleams but on the darkness of our prison
Whose chains and massy walls

We feel but cannot see.

'Spirit of Nature! all-sufficing Power,
Necessity! thou mother of the world!
Unlike the God of human error, thou
Requirest no prayers or praises; the caprice
Of man's weak will belongs no more to thee
Than do the changeful passions of his breast
To thy unvarying harmony; the slave,
Whose horrible lusts spread misery o'er the world,
And the good man, who lifts with virtuous pride
His being in the sight of happiness
That springs from his own works; the poison-tree,
Beneath whose shade all life is withered up,
And the fair oak, whose leafy dome affords
A temple where the vows of happy love
Are registered, are equal in thy sight;
No love, no hate thou cherishest; revenge
And favoritism, and worst desire of fame
Thou knowest not; all that the wide world contains
Are but thy passive instruments, and thou
Regard'st them all with an impartial eye,
Whose joy or pain thy nature cannot feel,
Because thou hast not human sense,
Because thou art not human mind.

'Yes! when the sweeping storm of time
Has sung its death-dirge o'er the ruined fanes
And broken altars of the almighty fiend,
Whose name usurps thy honors, and the blood
Through centuries clotted there has floated down
The tainted flood of ages, shalt thou live
Unchangeable! A shrine is raised to thee,
Which nor the tempest breath of time,
Nor the interminable flood
Over earth's slight pageant rolling,

Availeth to destroy, –
The sensitive extension of the world;
That wondrous and eternal fane,
Where pain and pleasure, good and evil join,
To do the will of strong necessity,
And life, in multitudinous shapes,
Still pressing forward where no term can be,
Like hungry and unresting flame
Curls round the eternal columns of its strength.'

VII.

SPIRIT

'I was an infant when my mother went
To see an atheist burned. She took me there.
The dark-robed priests were met around the pile;
The multitude was gazing silently;
And as the culprit passed with dauntless mien,
Tempered disdain in his unaltering eye,
Mixed with a quiet smile, shone calmly forth;
The thirsty fire crept round his manly limbs;
His resolute eyes were scorched to blindness soon;
His death-pang rent my heart! the insensate mob
Uttered a cry of triumph, and I wept.
"Weep not, child!" cried my mother, "for that man
Has said, There is no God."'

FAIRY

'There is no God!
Nature confirms the faith his death-groan sealed.
Let heaven and earth, let man's revolving race,
His ceaseless generations, tell their tale;
Let every part depending on the chain
That links it to the whole, point to the hand

That grasps its term! Let every seed that falls
In silent eloquence unfold its store
Of argument; infinity within,
Infinity without, belie creation;
The exterminable spirit it contains
Is Nature's only God; but human pride
Is skilful to invent most serious names
To hide its ignorance.
'the name of God
Has fenced about all crime with holiness,
Himself the creature of his worshippers,
Whose names and attributes and passions change,
Seeva, Buddh, Foh, Jehovah, God, or Lord,
Even with the human dupes who build his shrines,
Still serving o'er the war-polluted world
For desolation's watchword; whether hosts
Stain his death-blushing chariot-wheels, as on
Triumphantly they roll, whilst Brahmins raise
A sacred hymn to mingle with the groans;
Or countless partners of his power divide
His tyranny to weakness; or the smoke
Of burning towns, the cries of female helplessness,
Unarmed old age, and youth, and infancy,
Horribly massacred, ascend to heaven
In honor of his name; or, last and worst,
Earth groans beneath religion's iron age,
And priests dare babble of a God of peace,
Even whilst their hands are red with guiltless blood,
Murdering the while, uprooting every germ
Of truth, exterminating, spoiling all,
Making the earth a slaughter-house!

'O Spirit! through the sense
By which thy inner nature was apprised
Of outward shows, vague dreams have rolled,
And varied reminiscences have waked

Tablets that never fade;
All things have been imprinted there,
The stars, the sea, the earth, the sky,
Even the unshapeliest lineaments
Of wild and fleeting visions
Have left a record there
To testify of earth.

'These are my empire, for to me is given
The wonders of the human world to keep,
And fancy's thin creations to endow
With manner, being and reality;
Therefore a wondrous phantom from the dreams
Of human error's dense and purblind faith
I will evoke, to meet thy questioning.
Ahasuerus, rise!'

A strange and woe-worn wight
Arose beside the battlement,
And stood unmoving there.
His inessential figure cast no shade
Upon the golden floor;
His port and mien bore mark of many years,
And chronicles of untold ancientness
Were legible within his beamless eye;
Yet his cheek bore the mark of youth;
Freshness and vigor knit his manly frame;
The wisdom of old age was mingled there
With youth's primeval dauntlessness;
And inexpressible woe,
Chastened by fearless resignation, gave
An awful grace to his all-speaking brow.

SPIRIT

'Is there a God?'

AHASUERUS

'Is there a God! -ay, an almighty God,
And vengeful as almighty! Once his voice
Was heard on earth; earth shuddered at the sound;
The fiery-visaged firmament expressed
Abhorrence, and the grave of Nature yawned
To swallow all the dauntless and the good
That dared to hurl defiance at his throne,
Girt as it was with power. None but slaves
Survived, -cold-blooded slaves, who did the work
Of tyrannous omnipotence; whose souls
No honest indignation ever urged
To elevated daring, to one deed
Which gross and sensual self did not pollute.
These slaves built temples for the omnipotent fiend,
Gorgeous and vast; the costly altars smoked
With human blood, and hideous pæans rung
Through all the long-drawn aisles. A murderer heard
His voice in Egypt, one whose gifts and arts
Had raised him to his eminence in power,
Accomplice of omnipotence in crime
And confidant of the all-knowing one.
These were Jehovah's words.

'"From an eternity of idleness
I, God, awoke; in seven days' toil made earth
From nothing; rested, and created man;
I placed him in a paradise, and there
Planted the tree of evil, so that he
Might eat and perish, and my soul procure
Wherewith to sate its malice and to turn,
Even like a heartless conqueror of the earth,
All misery to my fame. The race of men,
Chosen to my honor, with impunity

May sate the lusts I planted in their heart.
Here I command thee hence to lead them on,
Until with hardened feet their conquering troops
Wade on the promised soil through woman's blood,
And make my name be dreaded through the land.
Yet ever-burning flame and ceaseless woe
Shall be the doom of their eternal souls,
With every soul on this ungrateful earth,
Virtuous or vicious, weak or strong, -even all
Shall perish, to fulfil the blind revenge
(Which you, to men, call justice) of their God."

'The murderer's brow
Quivered with horror.

'"God omnipotent,
Is there no mercy? must our punishment
Be endless? will long ages roll away,
And see no term? Oh! wherefore hast thou made
In mockery and wrath this evil earth?
Mercy becomes the powerful -be but just!
O God! repent and save!"

'"One way remains:
I will beget a son and he shall bear
The sins of all the world; he shall arise
In an unnoticed corner of the earth,
And there shall die upon a cross, and purge
The universal crime; so that the few
On whom my grace descends, those who are marked
As vessels to the honor of their God,
May credit this strange sacrifice and save
Their souls alive. Millions shall live and die,
Who ne'er shall call upon their Saviour's name,
But, unredeemed, go to the gaping grave,
Thousands shall deem it an old woman's tale,

Such as the nurses frighten babes withal;
These in a gulf of anguish and of flame
Shall curse their reprobation endlessly,
Yet tenfold pangs shall force them to avow,
Even on their beds of torment where they howl,
My honor and the justice of their doom.
What then avail their virtuous deeds, their thoughts
Of purity, with radiant genius bright
Or lit with human reason's earthly ray?
Many are called, but few will I elect.
Do thou my bidding, Moses!"

'Even the murderer's cheek
Was blanched with horror, and his quivering lips
Scarce faintly uttered -"O almighty one,
I tremble and obey!"

'O Spirit! centuries have set their seal
On this heart of many wounds, and loaded brain,
Since the Incarnate came; humbly he came,
Veiling his horrible Godhead in the shape
Of man, scorned by the world, his name unheard
Save by the rabble of his native town,
Even as a parish demagogue. He led
The crowd; he taught them justice, truth and peace,
In semblance; but he lit within their souls
The quenchless flames of zeal, and blessed the sword
He brought on earth to satiate with the blood
Of truth and freedom his malignant soul
At length his mortal frame was led to death.
I stood beside him; on the torturing cross
No pain assailed his unterrestrial sense;
And yet he groaned. Indignantly I summed
The massacres and miseries which his name
Had sanctioned in my country, and I cried,
"Go! go!" in mockery.

A smile of godlike malice reillumined
His fading lineaments. "I go," he cried,
"But thou shalt wander o'er the unquiet earth
Eternally." The dampness of the grave
Bathed my imperishable front. I fell,
And long lay tranced upon the charmèd soil.
When I awoke hell burned within my brain
Which staggered on its seat; for all around
The mouldering relics of my kindred lay,
Even as the Almighty's ire arrested them,
And in their various attitudes of death
My murdered children's mute and eyeless skulls
Glared ghastily upon me.

But my soul,
From sight and sense of the polluting woe
Of tyranny, had long learned to prefer
Hell's freedom to the servitude of heaven.
Therefore I rose, and dauntlessly began
My lonely and unending pilgrimage,
Resolved to wage unweariable war
With my almighty tyrant and to hurl
Defiance at his impotence to harm
Beyond the curse I bore. The very hand,
That barred my passage to the peaceful grave,
Has crushed the earth to misery, and given
Its empire to the chosen of his slaves.
These I have seen, even from the earliest dawn
Of weak, unstable and precarious power,
Then preaching peace, as now they practise war;
So, when they turned but from the massacre
Of unoffending infidels to quench
Their thirst for ruin in the very blood
That flowed in their own veins, and pitiless zeal
Froze every human feeling as the wife
Sheathed in her husband's heart the sacred steel,

Even whilst its hopes were dreaming of her love;
And friends to friends, brothers to brothers stood
Opposed in bloodiest battle-field, and war,
Scarce satiable by fate's last death-draught, waged,
Drunk from the wine-press of the Almighty's wrath;
Whilst the red cross, in mockery of peace,
Pointed to victory! When the fray was done,
No remnant of the exterminated faith
Survived to tell its ruin, but the flesh,
With putrid smoke poisoning the atmosphere,
That rotted on the half-extinguished pile.

'Yes! I have seen God's worshippers unsheathe
The sword of his revenge, when grace descended,
Confirming all unnatural impulses,
To sanctify their desolating deeds;
And frantic priests waved the ill-omened cross
O'er the unhappy earth; then shone the sun
On showers of gore from the upflashing steel
Of safe assassination, and all crime
Made stingless by the spirits of the Lord,
And blood-red rainbows canopied the land.

'Spirit! no year of my eventful being
Has passed unstained by crime and misery,
Which flows from God's own faith. I 've marked his slaves
With tongues, whose lies are venomous, beguile
The insensate mob, and, whilst one hand was red
With murder, feign to stretch the other out
For brotherhood and peace; and that they now
Babble of love and mercy, whilst their deeds
Are marked with all the narrowness and crime
That freedom's young arm dare not yet chastise,
Reason may claim our gratitude, who now,
Establishing the imperishable throne
Of truth and stubborn virtue, maketh vain

The unprevailing malice of my foe,
Whose bootless rage heaps torments for the brave,
Adds impotent eternities to pain,
Whilst keenest disappointment racks his breast
To see the smiles of peace around them play,
To frustrate or to sanctify their doom.

'Thus have I stood, -through a wild waste of years
Struggling with whirlwinds of mad agony,
Yet peaceful, and serene, and self-enshrined,
Mocking my powerless tyrant's horrible curse
With stubborn and unalterable will,
Even as a giant oak, which heaven's fierce flame
Had scathèd in the wilderness, to stand
A monument of fadeless ruin there;
Yet peacefully and movelessly it braves
The midnight conflict of the wintry storm,
As in the sunlight's calm it spreads
Its worn and withered arms on high
To meet the quiet of a summer's noon.'

The Fairy waved her wand;
Ahasuerus fled
Fast as the shapes of mingled shade and mist,
That lurk in the glens of a twilight grove,
Flee from the morning beam; -
The matter of which dreams are made
Not more endowed with actual life
Than this phantasmal portraiture
Of wandering human thought.

VIII.

THE FAIRY

'The present and the past thou hast beheld.

It was a desolate sight. Now, Spirit, learn,
The secrets of the future. -Time!
Unfold the brooding pinion of thy gloom,
Render thou up thy half-devoured babes,
And from the cradles of eternity,
Where millions lie lulled to their portioned sleep
By the deep murmuring stream of passing things,
Tear thou that gloomy shroud. -Spirit, behold
Thy glorious destiny!'

Joy to the Spirit came.
Through the wide rent in Time's eternal veil,
Hope was seen beaming through the mists of fear;
Earth was no longer hell;
Love, freedom, health had given
Their ripeness to the manhood of its prime,
And all its pulses beat
Symphonious to the planetary spheres;
Then dulcet music swelled
Concordant with the life-strings of the soul;
It throbbed in sweet and languid beatings there,
Catching new life from transitory death;
Like the vague sighings of a wind at even
That wakes the wavelets of the slumbering sea
And dies on the creation of its breath,
And sinks and rises, falls and swells by fits,
Was the pure stream of feeling
That sprung from these sweet notes,
And o'er the Spirit's human sympathies
With mild and gentle motion calmly flowed.

Joy to the Spirit came, -
Such joy as when a lover sees
The chosen of his soul in happiness
And witnesses her peace
Whose woe to him were bitterer than death;

Sees her unfaded cheek
Glow mantling in first luxury of health,
Thrills with her lovely eyes,
Which like two stars amid the heaving main
Sparkle through liquid bliss.

Then in her triumph spoke the Fairy Queen:
'I will not call the ghost of ages gone
To unfold the frightful secrets of its lore;
The present now is past,
And those events that desolate the earth
Have faded from the memory of Time,
Who dares not give reality to that
Whose being I annul. To me is given
The wonders of the human world to keep,
Space, matter, time and mind. Futurity
Exposes now its treasure; let the sight
Renew and strengthen all thy failing hope.
O human Spirit! spur thee to the goal
Where virtue fixes universal peace,
And, 'midst the ebb and flow of human things,
Show somewhat stable, somewhat certain still,
A light-house o'er the wild of dreary waves.

'The habitable earth is full of bliss;
Those wastes of frozen billows that were hurled
By everlasting snow-storms round the poles,
Where matter dared not vegetate or live,
But ceaseless frost round the vast solitude
Bound its broad zone of stillness, are unloosed;
And fragrant zephyrs there from spicy isles
Ruffle the placid ocean-deep, that rolls
Its broad, bright surges to the sloping sand,
Whose roar is wakened into echoings sweet
To murmur through the heaven-breathing groves
And melodize with man's blest nature there.

'Those deserts of immeasurable sand,
Whose age-collected fervors scarce allowed
A bird to live, a blade of grass to spring,
Where the shrill chirp of the green lizard's love
Broke on the sultry silentness alone,
Now teem with countless rills and shady woods,
Cornfields and pastures and white cottages;
And where the startled wilderness beheld
A savage conqueror stained in kindred blood,
A tigress sating with the flesh of lambs
The unnatural famine of her toothless cubs,
Whilst shouts and howlings through the desert rang, -
Sloping and smooth the daisy-spangled lawn,
Offering sweet incense to the sunrise, smiles
To see a babe before his mother's door,
Sharing his morning's meal
With the green and golden basilisk
That comes to lick his feet.

'Those trackless deeps, where many a weary sail
Has seen above the illimitable plain
Morning on night and night on morning rise,
Whilst still no land to greet the wanderer spread
Its shadowy mountains on the sun-bright sea,
Where the loud roarings of the tempest-waves
So long have mingled with the gusty wind
In melancholy loneliness, and swept
The desert of those ocean solitudes
But vocal to the sea-bird's harrowing shriek,
The bellowing monster, and the rushing storm;
Now to the sweet and many-mingling sounds
Of kindliest human impulses respond.
Those lonely realms bright garden-isles begem,
With lightsome clouds and shining seas between,
And fertile valleys, resonant with bliss,

Whilst green woods overcanopy the wave,
Which like a toil-worn laborer leaps to shore
To meet the kisses of the flowrets there.

'All things are recreated, and the flame
Of consentaneous love inspires all life.
The fertile bosom of the earth gives suck
To myriads, who still grow beneath her care,
Rewarding her with their pure perfectness;
The balmy breathings of the wind inhale
Her virtues and diffuse them all abroad;
Health floats amid the gentle atmosphere,
Glows in the fruits and mantles on the stream;
No storms deform the beaming brow of heaven,
Nor scatter in the freshness of its pride
The foliage of the ever-verdant trees;
But fruits are ever ripe, flowers ever fair,
And autumn proudly bears her matron grace,
Kindling a flush on the fair cheek of spring,
Whose virgin bloom beneath the ruddy fruit
Reflects its tint and blushes into love.

'The lion now forgets to thirst for blood;
There might you see him sporting in the sun
Beside the dreadless kid; his claws are sheathed,
His teeth are harmless, custom's force has made
His nature as the nature of a lamb.
Like passion's fruit, the nightshade's tempting bane
Poisons no more the pleasure it bestows;
All bitterness is past; the cup of joy
Unmingled mantles to the goblet's brim
And courts the thirsty lips it fled before.

But chief, ambiguous man, he that can know
More misery, and dream more joy than all;
Whose keen sensations thrill within his breast

To mingle with a loftier instinct there,
Lending their power to pleasure and to pain,
Yet raising, sharpening, and refining each;
Who stands amid the ever-varying world,
The burden or the glory of the earth;
He chief perceives the change; his being notes
The gradual renovation and defines
Each movement of its progress on his mind.

'Man, where the gloom of the long polar night
Lowers o'er the snow-clad rocks and frozen soil,
Where scarce the hardiest herb that braves the frost
Basks in the moonlight's ineffectual glow,
Shrank with the plants, and darkened with the night;
His chilled and narrow energies, his heart
Insensible to courage, truth or love,
His stunted stature and imbecile frame,
Marked him for some abortion of the earth,
Fit compeer of the bears that roamed around,
Whose habits and enjoyments were his own;
His life a feverish dream of stagnant woe,
Whose meagre wants, but scantily fulfilled,
Apprised him ever of the joyless length
Which his short being's wretchedness had reached;
His death a pang which famine, cold and toil
Long on the mind, whilst yet the vital spark
Clung to the body stubbornly, had brought:
All was inflicted here that earth's revenge
Could wreak on the infringers of her law;
One curse alone was spared -the name of God.

'Nor, where the tropics bound the realms of day
With a broad belt of mingling cloud and flame,
Where blue mists through the unmoving atmosphere
Scattered the seeds of pestilence and fed
Unnatural vegetation, where the land

Teemed with all earthquake, tempest and disease,
Was man a nobler being; slavery
Had crushed him to his country's blood-stained dust;
Or he was bartered for the fame of power,
Which, all internal impulses destroying,
Makes human will an article of trade;
Or he was changed with Christians for their gold
And dragged to distant isles, where to the sound
Of the flesh-mangling scourge he does the work
Of all-polluting luxury and wealth,
Which doubly visits on the tyrants' heads
The long-protracted fulness of their woe;
Or he was led to legal butchery,
To turn to worms beneath that burning sun
Where kings first leagued against the rights of men
And priests first traded with the name of God.

'Even where the milder zone afforded man
A seeming shelter, yet contagion there,
Blighting his being with unnumbered ills,
Spread like a quenchless fire; nor truth till late
Availed to arrest its progress or create
That peace which first in bloodless victory waved
Her snowy standard o'er this favored clime;
There man was long the train-bearer of slaves,
The mimic of surrounding misery,
The jackal of ambition's lion-rage,
The bloodhound of religion's hungry zeal.

'Here now the human being stands adorning
This loveliest earth with taintless body and mind;
Blest from his birth with all bland impulses,
Which gently in his noble bosom wake
All kindly passions and all pure desires.
Him, still from hope to hope the bliss pursuing
Which from the exhaustless store of human weal

Draws on the virtuous mind, the thoughts that rise
In time-destroying infiniteness gift
With self-enshrined eternity, that mocks
The unprevailing hoariness of age;
And man, once fleeting o'er the transient scene
Swift as an unremembered vision, stands
Immortal upon earth; no longer now
He slays the lamb that looks him in the face,
And horribly devours his mangled flesh,
Which, still avenging Nature's broken law,
Kindled all putrid humors in his frame,
All evil passions and all vain belief,
Hatred, despair and loathing in his mind,
The germs of misery, death, disease and crime.
No longer now the wingèd habitants,
That in the woods their sweet lives sing away,
Flee from the form of man; but gather round,
And prune their sunny feathers on the hands
Which little children stretch in friendly sport
Towards these dreadless partners of their play.
All things are void of terror; man has lost
His terrible prerogative, and stands
An equal amidst equals; happiness
And science dawn, though late, upon the earth;
Peace cheers the mind, health renovates the frame;
Disease and pleasure cease to mingle here,
Reason and passion cease to combat there;
Whilst each unfettered o'er the earth extend
Their all-subduing energies, and wield
The sceptre of a vast dominion there;
Whilst every shape and mode of matter lends
Its force to the omnipotence of mind,
Which from its dark mine drags the gem of truth
To decorate its paradise of peace.'

IX.

'O happy Earth, reality of Heaven!
To which those restless souls that ceaselessly
Throng through the human universe, aspire!
Thou consummation of all mortal hope!
Thou glorious prize of blindly working will,
Whose rays, diffused throughout all space and time,
Verge to one point and blend forever there!
Of purest spirits thou pure dwelling-place
Where care and sorrow, impotence and crime,
Languor, disease and ignorance dare not come!
O happy Earth, reality of Heaven!

'Genius has seen thee in her passionate dreams;
And dim forebodings of thy loveliness,
Haunting the human heart, have there entwined
Those rooted hopes of some sweet place of bliss,
Where friends and lovers meet to part no more.
Thou art the end of all desire and will,
The product of all action; and the souls,
That by the paths of an aspiring change
Have reached thy haven of perpetual peace,
There rest from the eternity of toil
That framed the fabric of thy perfectness.

'Even Time, the conqueror, fled thee in his fear;
That hoary giant, who in lonely pride
So long had ruled the world that nations fell
Beneath his silent footstep. Pyramids,
That for millenniums had withstood the tide
Of human things, his storm-breath drove in sand
Across that desert where their stones survived
The name of him whose pride had heaped them there.
Yon monarch, in his solitary pomp,
Was but the mushroom of a summer day,
That his light-wingèd footstep pressed to dust;

Time was the king of earth; all things gave way
Before him but the fixed and virtuous will,
The sacred sympathies of soul and sense,
That mocked his fury and prepared his fall.

'Yet slow and gradual dawned the morn of love;
Long lay the clouds of darkness o'er the scene,
Till from its native heaven they rolled away:
First, crime triumphant o'er all hope careered
Unblushing, undisguising, bold and strong,
Whilst falsehood, tricked in virtue's attributes,
Long sanctified all deeds of vice and woe,
Till, done by her own venomous sting to death,
She left the moral world without a law,
No longer fettering passion's fearless wing,
Nor searing reason with the brand of God.
Then steadily the happy ferment worked;
Reason was free; and wild though passion went
Through tangled glens and wood-embosomed meads,
Gathering a garland of the strangest flowers,
Yet, like the bee returning to her queen,
She bound the sweetest on her sister's brow,
Who meek and sober kissed the sportive child,
No longer trembling at the broken rod.

'Mild was the slow necessity of death.
The tranquil spirit failed beneath its grasp,
Without a groan, almost without a fear,
Calm as a voyager to some distant land,
And full of wonder, full of hope as he.
The deadly germs of languor and disease
Died in the human frame, and purity
Blessed with all gifts her earthly worshippers.
How vigorous then the athletic form of age!
How clear its open and unwrinkled brow!
Where neither avarice, cunning, pride or care

Had stamped the seal of gray deformity
On all the mingling lineaments of time.
How lovely the intrepid front of youth,
Which meek-eyed courage decked with freshest grace;
Courage of soul, that dreaded not a name,
And elevated will, that journeyed on
Through life's phantasmal scene in fearlessness,
With virtue, love and pleasure, hand in hand!

'Then, that sweet bondage which is freedom's self,
And rivets with sensation's softest tie
The kindred sympathies of human souls,
Needed no fetters of tyrannic law.
Those delicate and timid impulses
In Nature's primal modesty arose,
And with undoubting confidence disclosed
The growing longings of its dawning love,
Unchecked by dull and selfish chastity,
That virtue of the cheaply virtuous,
Who pride themselves in senselessness and frost.
No longer prostitution's venomed bane
Poisoned the springs of happiness and life;
Woman and man, in confidence and love,
Equal and free and pure together trod
The mountain-paths of virtue, which no more
Were stained with blood from many a pilgrim's feet.

'Then, where, through distant ages, long in pride
The palace of the monarch-slave had mocked
Famine's faint groan and penury's silent tear,
A heap of crumbling ruins stood, and threw
Year after year their stones upon the field,
Wakening a lonely echo; and the leaves
Of the old thorn, that on the topmost tower
Usurped the royal ensign's grandeur, shook
In the stern storm that swayed the topmost tower,

And whispered strange tales in the whirlwind's ear.

'Low through the lone cathedral's roofless aisles
The melancholy winds a death-dirge sung.
It were a sight of awfulness to see
The works of faith and slavery, so vast,
So sumptuous, yet so perishing withal,
Even as the corpse that rests beneath its wall!
A thousand mourners deck the pomp of death
To-day, the breathing marble glows above
To decorate its memory, and tongues
Are busy of its life; to-morrow, worms
In silence and in darkness seize their prey.

'Within the massy prison's mouldering courts,
Fearless and free the ruddy children played,
Weaving gay chaplets for their innocent brows
With the green ivy and the red wall-flower
That mock the dungeon's unavailing gloom;
The ponderous chains and gratings of strong iron
There rusted amid heaps of broken stone
That mingled slowly with their native earth;
There the broad beam of day, which feebly once
Lighted the cheek of lean captivity
With a pale and sickly glare, then freely shone
On the pure smiles of infant playfulness;
No more the shuddering voice of hoarse despair
Pealed through the echoing vaults, but soothing notes
Of ivy-fingered winds and gladsome birds
And merriment were resonant around.

'These ruins soon left not a wreck behind;
Their elements, wide-scattered o'er the globe,
To happier shapes were moulded, and became
Ministrant to all blissful impulses;
Thus human things were perfected, and earth,

Even as a child beneath its mother's love,
Was strengthened in all excellence, and grew
Fairer and nobler with each passing year.

'Now Time his dusky pennons o'er the scene
Closes in steadfast darkness, and the past
Fades from our charmèd sight. My task is done;
Thy lore is learned. Earth's wonders are thine own
With all the fear and all the hope they bring.
My spells are passed; the present now recurs.
Ah me! a pathless wilderness remains
Yet unsubdued by man's reclaiming hand.

'Yet, human Spirit! bravely hold thy course;
Let virtue teach thee firmly to pursue
The gradual paths of an aspiring change;
For birth and life and death, and that strange state
Before the naked soul has found its home,
All tend to perfect happiness, and urge
The restless wheels of being on their way,
Whose flashing spokes, instinct with infinite life,
Bicker and burn to gain their destined goal;
For birth but wakes the spirit to the sense
Of outward shows, whose unexperienced shape
New modes of passion to its frame may lend;
Life is its state of action, and the store
Of all events is aggregated there
That variegate the eternal universe;
Death is a gate of dreariness and gloom,
That leads to azure isles and beaming skies
And happy regions of eternal hope.
Therefore, O Spirit! fearlessly bear on.
Though storms may break the primrose on its stalk,
Though frosts may blight the freshness of its bloom,
Yet spring's awakening breath will woo the earth
To feed with kindliest dews its favorite flower,

That blooms in mossy bank and darksome glens,
Lighting the greenwood with its sunny smile.

'Fear not then, Spirit, death's disrobing hand,
So welcome when the tyrant is awake,
So welcome when the bigot's hell-torch burns;
't is but the voyage of a darksome hour,
The transient gulf-dream of a startling sleep.
Death is no foe to virtue; earth has seen
Love's brightest roses on the scaffold bloom,
Mingling with freedom's fadeless laurels there,
And presaging the truth of visioned bliss.
Are there not hopes within thee, which this scene
Of linked and gradual being has confirmed?
Whose stingings bade thy heart look further still,
When, to the moonlight walk by Henry led,
Sweetly and sadly thou didst talk of death?
And wilt thou rudely tear them from thy breast,
Listening supinely to a bigot's creed,
Or tamely crouching to the tyrant's rod,
Whose iron thongs are red with human gore?
Never: but bravely bearing on, thy will
Is destined an eternal war to wage
With tyranny and falsehood, and uproot
The germs of misery from the human heart.
Thine is the hand whose piety would soothe
The thorny pillow of unhappy crime,
Whose impotence an easy pardon gains,
Watching its wanderings as a friend's disease;
Thine is the brow whose mildness would defy
Its fiercest rage, and brave its sternest will,
When fenced by power and master of the world.
Thou art sincere and good; of resolute mind,
Free from heart-withering custom's cold control,
Of passion lofty, pure and unsubdued.
Earth's pride and meanness could not vanquish thee,

And therefore art thou worthy of the boon
Which thou hast now received; virtue shall keep
Thy footsteps in the path that thou hast trod,
And many days of beaming hope shall bless
Thy spotless life of sweet and sacred love.
Go, happy one, and give that bosom joy,
Whose sleepless spirit waits to catch
Light, life and rapture from thy smile!'

The Fairy waves her wand of charm.
Speechless with bliss the Spirit mounts the car,
That rolled beside the battlement,
Bending her beamy eyes in thankfulness.
Again the enchanted steeds were yoked;
Again the burning wheels inflame
The steep descent of heaven's untrodden way.
Fast and far the chariot flew;
The vast and fiery globes that rolled
Around the Fairy's palace-gate
Lessened by slow degrees, and soon appeared
Such tiny twinklers as the planet orbs
That there attendant on the solar power
With borrowed light pursued their narrower way.

Earth floated then below;
The chariot paused a moment there;
The Spirit then descended;
The restless coursers pawed the ungenial soil,
Snuffed the gross air, and then, their errand done,
Unfurled their pinions to the winds of heaven.

The Body and the Soul united then.
A gentle start convulsed Ianthe's frame;
Her veiny eyelids quietly unclosed;
Moveless awhile the dark blue orbs remained.
She looked around in wonder, and beheld

Henry, who kneeled in silence by her couch,
Watching her sleep with looks of speechless love,
And the bright beaming stars
That through the casement shone.

Bio: Percy Bysshe Shelley was one of the major English Romantic poets, and is regarded by critics as amongst the finest lyric poets in the English language.

THE HUNTING OF THE DRAGON

G.K. Chesterton

When we went hunting the Dragon
In the days when we were young,
We tossed the bright world over our shoulder
As bugle and baldrick slung;
Never was world so wild and fair
As what went by on the wind,
Never such fields of paradise
As the fields we left behind:
For this is the best of a rest for men
That men should rise and ride
Making a flying fairyland
Of market and country-side,
Wings on the cottage, wings on the wood,
Wings upon pot and pan,
For the hunting of the Dragon
That is the life of a man.

For men grow weary of fairyland
When the Dragon is a dream,
And tire of the talking bird in the tree,
The singing fish in the stream;
And the wandering stars grow stale, grow stale,
And the wonder is stiff with scorn;
For this is the honour of fairyland
And the following of the horn;

Beauty on beauty called us back

When we could rise and ride,
And a woman looked out of every window
As wonderful as a bride:
And the tavern-sign as a tabard blazed,
And the children cheered and ran,
For the love of the hate of the Dragon
That is the pride of a man.

The sages called him a shadow
And the light went out of the sun:
And the wise men told us that all was well
And all was weary and one:
And then, and then, in the quiet garden,
With never a weed to kill,
We knew that his shining tail had shone
In the white road over the hill:
We knew that the clouds were flakes of flame,
We knew that the sunset fire
Was red with the blood of the Dragon
Whose death is the world's desire.

For the horn was blown in the heart of the night
That men should rise and ride,
Keeping the tryst of a terrible jest
Never for long untried;
Drinking a dreadful blood for wine,
Never in cup or can,
The death of a deathless Dragon,
That is the life of a man.

Bio: Gilbert Keith Chesterton, KC*SG better known as G. K. Chesterton, was an English writer, lay theologian, poet, philosopher, dramatist, journalist, orator, literary and art critic, biographer, and Christian apologist.

THE NATURE OF SPECULATIVE POETRY AND THE FANTASTIC

In his book The Fantastic: A Structural Approach to a Literary Genre (1975), Tzvetan Todorov offers the following definitions of fantastic literature:

"In a world which is indeed our world, the one we know....there occurs an event which cannot be explained by the laws of this same familiar world. The person who experiences the event must opt for one of two possible solutions: either he is the victim of an illusion of the senses, of a product of the imagination-- and the laws of the world then remain what they are; or else the event has indeed taken place, it is an integral part of reality--but then this reality is controlled by laws unknown to us (p. 25)."

"The fantastic occupies the duration of this uncertainty....The fantastic is that hesitation experienced by a person who knows only the laws of nature, confronting an apparently supernatural event (p. 25)."

Todorov later comments:

"The fantastic requires the fulfillment of three conditions. First, the text must oblige the reader to consider the world of the characters as a world of living persons and to hesitate between a natural or supernatural explanation of the events described. Second, this hesitation may also be experienced by a character; thus the reader's role is so to speak entrusted to a character, and at the same time the hesitation is represented, it becomes one of the themes of the work--in the case of naive reading, the actual reader identifies himself with the character. Third, the reader must adopt a certain attitude with regard to the text: he will reject allegorical as well as "poetic" interpretations (p. 33)."

Todorov distinguishes the fantastic from two other modes, the uncanny and the marvelous. While these modes have some of the ambiguity of the fantastic, they ultimately offer a resolution governed by natural laws (the uncanny) or the supernatural (the marvelous).

"[In the uncanny], events are related which may be readily accounted for by the laws of reason, but which are, in one way or another, incredible, extraordinary, shocking, singular, disturbing or unexpected, and which thereby provoke in the character and in the reader a reaction similar to that which works of the fantastic have made familiar (p. 46)." Todorov's definition of the uncanny might be applied to stories in which the character realizes s/he is mad or has just awakened from a dream. Thus, the uncanny is an "experience of limits."

"If we move to the other side of that median line which we have called the fantastic, we find ourselves in the fantastic-marvelous, the class of narratives that are presented as fantastic and that end with an acceptance of the supernatural (p. 52)."

From such early allegorical texts such as Edmund Spenser's Faerie Queene to modern works like J. K. Rowling's "Harry Potter" series, writers have used the fantastic element in novels, poetry, and short stories. The use of the fantastic as a literary element in books, poems, and drama has been a consistent trend across many genres and over many centuries. In the twentieth century in particular, fantasy assumed a central place in literature, specifically as a structural and allegorical element that has allowed authors from varied backgrounds to tell their stories to a universal audience.

E.E. Cummings suggests, "feeling is first who pays any attention to the syntax of things." According to Cummings, poetry is purely defined by the feelings the poem expresses and syntax plays no role. This is evident when he writes "for life's not a paragraph And death I think is no parenthesis." While poetry must express feelings and must create "imaginary gardens with real toads in them." Poetry cannot be defined by these standards alone. After all, without certain rules to define poetry any expression of emotion can be defined as poetry. While it is true that the main purpose of poetry is to create worlds and express emotions, poetry must also accomplish more.

Dealing with the fantastic as opposed to the mundane, speculative poetry travels winding roads leading to wondrous worlds, regions never traversed by mainstream verse. Fantastic poems range in the material they treat from the strange but explainable to the utterly fanciful, from horror to wonder, and from the rigidly verisimilitudinous to the purely surrealist. They may utilize traditional prosody or may avail themselves of the discontinuities and fragmentation of modernist free verse. They may use as setting the primary world, a secondary world, or a combination of the two. With roots planted firmly in the mythic and folkloric epics and ballads of yore, and branches reaching high into the endless skies of modern fantasy, science fiction, and horror, speculative poetry is a historic and vital poetic genre.

The impact of the fantastic relies on the fact that the world presented in these stories seems to be real, yet everything is different. This discontinuity and disconnect imbues each phrase and all images in the text with layers of meanings and associations that almost create a new language. While a number of critics view the use of the fantastic as an effective means of confronting issues that are important in reality, an equal number of critics and authors believe in the sustaining power of fantasy because of the escape and release it provides.

Literature dealing with the fantastic routinely deals with issues of sociological and theological significance. The most powerful fantasies operate on a dual level, using a combination of allegory and literal meaning to explore recognizable and pertinent human conflicts in a setting that is imaginative and extraordinary.

OTHER TITLES BY DREAMSCAPE PRESS

100 Worlds: Lightning-Quick SF & Fantasy Tales

100 authors from across the galaxy tackle the experimental art of drabble. Featuring Milo James Fowler, Cheryl A. Warner, Stephen Sottong, Jason Lairamore, Theodore Kanbe, Von Rupert, Robert Lowell Russell, Simon Kewin, Chuck Von Nordheim, Carly Berg, Chris White, Lance Manion, and others.

$9.21. 118pp. 149355058X.

Haiku of the Dead

Poetry to eat your brains. An anthology that pieces together a warm-hearted story of guts and gore. Told through the imagistic language of haiku, every flesh-ripping moment of the zombie apocalypse is covered, from dawn to demise. Thirty-five narrators take the readers through infested streets and graveyards from the points of view of both survivors and the undead. Featuring Jason Kirk, Colin W. Campbell, Jessica McHugh, and others.

$8.99. 48pp. 1495262286.

Contact: Stories of the New World

A cast of authors from past, present and future make up this collection of eighteen stories featuring original works and classic reprints. Contact: Stories of the New World takes you beyond the edge of the solar system into the uncharted horizons of deep space, where the spaces and dimensions in between are explored and worlds of mystery are discovered. Featuring Chris Limb, Damien Krsteski, HG Wells, Jason Andrew, Kurt Heinrich Hyat, Margaret Karmazin, Philip K Dick, Tom Barlow, and others.

$14.99. 246pp. 1494386356.

Nuclear-Town USA

There will come a time when everything we know and love will cease to exist. But how will such a disaster transpire - by nuclear warfare, ecological collapse,

technological failure, perhaps pandemic? And how would we cope in our last hours, in catastrophe's wake? This theme of finality is explored in Nuclear Town USA, a collection of apocalyptic and dystopian fiction set across a diversity of scenarios and backdrops. From fast-paced thrillers to dark reflections, each story intriguingly captures frightening alt-realities surrounding humanity's twilight. Featuring Adam Millard, Eryk Pruitt, Damien Krsteski, Jesse Harlin, Jon Alston, and others.
$14.99. 162pp. 1494346893.

Cosmic Vegetable

Cats, six-breasted nymphs, space zombies, talking furries, romantic weaboos, sexy slime dancers, an over-eating insectavore, an uxorious time-bending physicist, thoughtful social commentary, fart jokes, and, of course, mobbins. A humorous science fiction and fantasy anthology with the following side effects : incessant smiling, muscle aches, laugh fits, stomach aches, crying, depression, wetting oneself, blindness, demonic possession, and finally, death by laugh-induced asphyxiation. Featuring Adam Millard, Deborah Walker, Erik Gern, Fred Russell, James Aquilone, James S. Dorr, Margaret Karmazin, and others.
$14.99. 250pp. 1494340984.

Clockwork Kiru: Steampunk Haiku

In a world that never was but should have been, steam rules the sea, the skies and the aether. Amid a cacophony of cranking sprockets and cogs, in chuffs of steam and soot, "Clockwork Kiru: Steampunk Haiku" looks to the future through the lens of the past - through the imagistic language of haiku. In this anthology of steampunk haiku, fifty authors take the reader on a fantastical, around-the-world adventure with haiku seeped in mystery, magic, science and romance. Featuring E.S. Wynn, Deborah Walker, Jo Wu, Tyson West, Mercedes Webb-Pullman, Narendra Daivari, and others.
$9.99. 68pp. 1502773481.

We've published all these writers and more:

Adam Millard, Cheryl A. Warner, Damien Krstenski, Deborah Walker, Eryk Pruitt, James Aquilone, James S. Dorr, Jason Lairamore, Margaret Karmazin, Milo James Fowler, Richard Jay Goldstein, Robert Lowell Russell, Simon Kewin , Stephen Sottong, Theodore Kanbe!

Visit us online to see our complete catalogue:

http://dreamscapepress.wordpress.com
http://www.twitter.com/dreamscapepress

Books Available At All Leading Paperback Retailers!

Made in the USA
Monee, IL
22 September 2020